D0546148

Scottish

SCOTTISH BATTLES

Scottish Histories

SCOTTISH BATTLES

J. HAMILTON

WAVERLEY
BOOKS

Published 2008 by Geddes & Grosset,
David Dale House, New Lanark, ML11 9DJ, Scotland

Copyright © Geddes & Grosset 2004

ISBN 978 1 902407 70 8

Printed in India

CONTENTS

FOREWORD

The many tensions that existed among the Scots, their invaders, and their neighbours down the centuries often led to bloody conflict. Warfare became part of Scotland's history and culture.

Over time, many battles have been fought within and without Scotland's boundaries, from internal clashes between warring clans to the great battles of the 18th century. Victory was often elusive but even in defeat, the Scots were an enemy to be feared whose fierce courage in battle struck terror in the hearts of their enemies.

In the pages that follow, the most important of these battles are described in some detail and their place in Scotland's history explained.

PART I:
INVASIONS AND POWER STRUGGLES

BATTLE OF MONS GRAUPIUS, 84CE

Agricola's campaign in Scotland

The battle of Mons Graupius, between the forces of the Roman governor Gnaeus Julius Agricola and the Caledonians led by Calgacus, is the first Scottish battle about which there is any substantial documentary evidence available to historians. Most of what is known about the battle comes from the writings of the Roman historian Tacitus, in his work on Agricola. Tacitus was married to Agricola's daughter.

Agricola was appointed governor in Britain in 78CE, and whilst continuing a programme of romanisation in the south, he swiftly moved to subdue northern England, before turning his attentions to Scotland.

Agricola first crossed into Scotland in 80CE, hoping to extend the boundaries of Roman control from the south. In that year, his forces encountered no form of organised opposition and he was able to construct a number of forts in the newly subdued territories. By the end of the second year, he had constructed a line of forts between the Forth and the Clyde, connected to the south by a road over the Pentlands and the Cheviots, also heavily fortified. He had also constructed and manned a number of forts on the route to the north. Having thus established a strong position south of the Forth–Clyde isthmus, he set about advancing further north in 83CE. His land forces, a combination of Roman legionaries and auxiliary forces from other parts of the Roman empire, had the additional support of a sizable naval force which travelled up the coast, keeping pace with the land forces, and attacking and pillaging coastal settlements as they went.

For most of the year, Agricola's forces continued the move north. Although the Roman forces were not drawn into any major battles during this period, there were signs that the Caledonians were preparing to resist their advances with greater ferocity than they had previously shown. A series of attacks on Roman forts hampered the progress of the Roman army, and Agricola took the decision to split his forces in three in order to avoid the danger of becoming hemmed in by the enemy. The Caledonians became aware of this, and took advantage. A surprise night attack by the Caledonians nearly overwhelmed the men of the ninth legion, but help arrived at the last minute and the Caledonians scattered.

The Romans took a break from the campaign during the winter of 83–84CE, in the fort of Inchtuthil in Perthshire. As the weather grew warmer, Agricola prepared to advance further and in late summer, the Roman forces moved on. During the winter months when the Roman army had been relatively inactive, the Caledonian tribes had organised themselves into a solid body of resistance, under the leadership of Calgacus. As Agricola's army moved into the Grampians, the Caledonians were preparing to meet the invaders with an army of more than 30,000 men. The Caledonians waited for the invaders on the lower slopes of Mons Graupius.

The battle of Mons Graupius

The exact location of Mons Graupius has not been proven beyond all doubt, but it is thought to be at Bennachie, a hill to the northwest of Aberdeen.

The sight of the assembled enemy warriors must have been intimidating for the Roman governor. His men, although a better trained and more cohesive fighting force, were outnumbered by the Caledonians, who had added to their advantage by positioning most of their men on higher ground. The front line of the Caledonian horde was on low ground, backed by an assembly of charioteers and cavalry. Behind these two lines, the rest of the Caledonians were arranged in closely packed tiers up the hillside. Agricola drew up his own battle plan, and arranged his men ready for the encounter. He only had two Roman legions with him, the ninth and the twentieth. The rest of his army was composed of auxiliary forces. Deciding it was better not to risk his finest men first, he placed the legionaries behind the auxiliary troops. He placed his auxiliary infantry (mostly German cohorts) in the middle at the front, and divided the auxiliary cavalry between the eastern and western flanks. In order to avoid the possibility of being outflanked by the Caledonians, he spread the battle line wide and thin.

Before battle commenced, Tacitus tells us, both leaders gave motivational speeches to their assembled troops. It might reasonably be argued that Tacitus's account of the encounter would be coloured both by his own nationality and by his relationship to Agricola, for whom, from the tone of his writing, he had a great respect. But the speech that Tacitus puts into the mouth of Calgacus shows that the historian was prepared to show considerable insight into the Roman campaign as seen from the perspective of the Caledonians. Tacitus presents Calgacus as a brave and inspirational leader who tells his men they are faced with a choice between fighting for freedom and submitting to slavery. Of the Romans, Tacitus has Calgacus say:

Robbers of the world, having by their universal plunder exhausted the land, they rifle the deep. If the enemy be rich, they are rapacious; if he be poor, they lust for dominion. Neither the east nor the west has been able to satisfy them. Alone among men they covet with equal eagerness poverty and riches. To robbery, slaughter and plunder, they give the lying name of empire; they make a solitude and call it peace.

The battle began with an exchange of arrows and missiles from both sides. Then Agricola ordered five of the auxiliary cohorts, Batavians and Tungrians, to advance and engage the enemy in hand-to-hand fighting with swords. The Caledonians' swords were unwieldy; they were long and had no point, and were thus not well suited to close combat. Armed with smaller, sharper weapons and strong shields, the Batavians and Tungrians inflicted terrible damage upon their opponents. The other auxiliary forces joined in the affray, and a number of cavalrymen. Panic spread among the Caledonians, as their charioteers lost control of their horses or were slain, and unmanned chariots careered around in the throng, adding to the carnage. The Caledonians were being pushed further back up the lower slopes of the hill. Then Agricola noticed some of the forces that had been ranged on the higher slopes begin to move out and down, as if to pass the Roman forces on either side before attacking them from the rear. Agricola sent more cavalry to meet them and fight them off. The counter-manoeuvre was successful, and the Roman cavalry moved on and round to the back of the Caledonian forces. With Romans in front and Romans behind, the Caledonians were thrown into total disarray. Many of them, seeing the hopelessness of their situation, fled for the safety of the forests. Those who stayed to fight were slain. Those who had fled to the forest regrouped and launched a second assault upon the pursuing Roman troops, only to be put to flight when Agricola sent both infantry and cavalry after them, sweeping through the trees in an unforgiving line.

The night was spent in the recovery of the wounded. Next day, there was not a sign of the retreating Caledonians. They had carried away their wounded, burned their houses and disappeared into the wilds.

The battle of Mons Graupius was not, as Agricola might have hoped, the beginning of the complete subjugation of the wild Caledonians. Agricola's navy continued its journey around the coast of Scotland, and it was established beyond doubt that Britain was an island. But there were to be no more great military victories, no further conquests. Agricola was recalled to Rome the following year and the forts in the north were abandoned. The Caledonian tribes fought their way southwards to the Roman frontier. In 122CE, construction began on Hadrian's Wall, to keep the marauding Caledonians at bay. Twenty years later, Antonine's Wall was built between the Forth and the Clyde and its forts manned by auxiliary forces from Gaul, Thrace, Germany and Syria, to bolster further the Roman defences against invasion from the north. But the uprisings continued and repeated rebuilding and reinforcement of the defences began to fail. Around 183CE, the Romans finally gave up hope of retaining any sort of hold on Scotland, and abandoned all forts north of Hadrian's Wall. A last-ditch attempt to subdue the northern tribes was carried out in 208CE by the emperor, Septimus Severus. His achievements were at great human cost and were short-lived. In 211CE, Septimus Severus died, and with him, Rome's last hope of conquering Scotland.

BATTLE OF BRUNANBURH, 937CE

Scotland in the ninth and tenth centuries

In the centuries that followed the departure of the Romans, the lands of the Caledonian tribes, or the Picts as they are more commonly known, underwent great change. By the ninth century, the territory now known as Scotland was divided into five distinct areas. In the fifth century, the Scots, Celtic people from the northeast of Ireland, had landed on the northwest coast of Scotland and had established the kingdom of Dàl Riada. The land between the Tweed and the Forth was occupied by Angles, who had invaded from the south. The southwest of the country was the home of the Strathclyde Britons. The land to the east of Dàl Riada and north of the Forth belonged to the Picts. And from the second half of the eighth century onwards, Norsemen, invaders and settlers from Denmark and Norway, began to establish themselves in Orkney and the Hebrides.

In 839, following the death of Eoganan, king of the Picts, in battle against the Norsemen, the kingdoms of the Scots and the Picts were united under one ruler, Kenneth MacAlpin. The unified kingdom became known as Alba. But the peace that might have been brought by this unification was continually threatened by the raids of the Norsemen. Kenneth was succeeded by his brother Donald, who reigned from 860 to 864. After Donald's death, his nephew Constantine came to the throne, and a period of almost continual conflict with the

Norsemen began. Danes invaded from Ireland in 866 and caused devastation in Constantine's kingdom. They came again in 867, and this time were successfully repulsed, but turned their attentions to Strathclyde, in successive attacks destroying Dumbarton, the capital, and taking a great number of captives. Then, between 875 and 877, Constantine's kingdom was ravaged yet again in a series of attacks. Constantine died in 877, fighting against the Norwegians. The fighting continued almost continually over the next 23 years, through the reigns of Aed, his brother (ruled 877–878), Giric, his nephew (ruled 878–889), and Donald II, his son (ruled 889–900). Donald II died in 900, slain in battle against the Norsemen at Dunnottar, and his successor was Constantine II, son of Aed.

In Constantine II's reign, which was to last much longer than that of any of his recent predecessors (900–943), the situation changed. The Norsemen continued attacking Alba and Strathclyde. They sacked Dunkeld, religious centre of the Scots kingdom, in 903, but were repelled at Strathearn in 904. Further south a few years later, the Danes were threatening Northumberland, and Constantine led his men south to support King Aldred against them. Constantine and Aldred were both fortunate to escape with their lives, but Northumberland was taken and the Danes settled there.

Then in 926, Sihtric, the king of the Danes in Northumberland, died and Athelstan, king of Wessex and Mercia, drove Sihtric's two sons, Godfrey and Olaf, out. Godfrey sought refuge with Constantine, and Constantine made him welcome. This was the first sign of a change in allegiance on Constantine's part and it angered Athelstan. When Constantine gave his daughter in marriage to Olaf, Sihtric's other son, it became clear to Athelstan that he could no longer expect Constantine to side with him against the Norsemen. In 934, fearing that Constantine was now forming an alliance with the Britons and the Norsemen to make war against him,

Athelstan attacked by both sea and land. His fleet plundered the east coast, and land forces attacked the Britons in Strathclyde, and the land of the Scots, plundering and pillaging in a tremendous show of force. Constantine was humiliated; but he was not ready to admit utter defeat.

The battle of Brunanburh

The exact location of the battle of Brunanburh is not known, but it is thought to be Birrenswark, in Dumfries and Galloway. A poem giving an account of it survives in the *Anglo-Saxon Chronicle*. The poem presents the English as a united and courageous body of men, determined to drive out the invader at all costs. The battle is recorded as the worst in terms of killing since the Angles and Saxons first invaded the shores of England.

In 937, Olaf, Constantine's son-in-law, came from Ireland with a fleet of ships and a great number of men. Constantine met them in the Solway with his own fleet and they landed together and joined up with Owen, leader of the Strathclyde Britons, and his body of men. Hearing that an attack was imminent, Athelstan led his army north immediately and met them at Brunanburh. The fight went on from dawn till dusk. It was a struggle marked by desperate heroism on both sides. The English suffered massive losses as they charged against the enemy shields repeatedly, while their archers kept firing a rain of arrows on the Scots and Norsemen. At last the persistence of the English began to pay off and the enemy lines began to disintegrate. The English moved forward again and the invaders began to retreat, to the north, or to the west and the safety of their ships. As the English harried them into flight, the bodies of their dead littered the battleground, waiting for the carrion-eaters to fight over their flesh.

The massive defeat marked the end of Constantine's reign. He was an old man now, weak in body and diminished in spirit. He retired to a monastery, and Malcolm I, son of Donald II, took his place as king. The battle had cost the Scots a great deal. There were no more threats to Athelstan's kingdom until after his death, three years later.

BATTLE OF DURHAM, 1006

Malcolm II

The tenth century was a period marked for the kings of Alba by internal feuding over the succession to the throne, territorial disputes with the English and Strathclyde Britons, and renewed attacks by the Norse invaders. Between 937 and 1005, eight kings ruled over Alba. They were Malcolm I (943–954), Indulf, son of Constantine II (954–962), Dub, son of Malcolm I (962–967), Culen, son of Indulf (967–971), Kenneth II, son of Malcolm I (971–995), Constantine III, son of Culen (995–997), Kenneth III, son of Dub (?)(997–?), and Girigc, son of Kenneth III (?–1005).

In 1005, Malcolm II, son of Kenneth II, came to the throne after having killed his predecessor, Girigc, in battle at Monzievard near the River Earn. He ruled for 29 years, and proved to be a capable warrior king.

The battle of Durham

In 1006, Malcolm advanced into England with an army, and plundering and burning on his route south, arrived at Durham and put it under siege. A force led by Uhtred of Northumberland launched a vicious assault on Malcolm's army and the king was lucky to escape with his life. Durham was the only serious defeat of Malcolm's reign.

BATTLE OF CLONTARF, 1014

In 1014, an army of Scots fought with the Irish under King Brian Bòruma at the battle of Clontarf in Ireland against the Norsemen. The Norsemen were defeated and Sigurd, who ruled over Orkney and also Caithness, Ross, Sutherland, and Moray, was killed. The battle marked the end of Norse rule over Ireland, and also brought benefits for Scotland, where the Norse hold on the mainland had now been weakened. Malcolm conferred Orkney, Caithness, and Sutherland on Thorfinn, a son of Sigurd who had married his daughter, and made Finnlaec, husband of his other daughter Donada, mormaer of Moray.

BATTLE OF CARHAM, 1018

In 1018, Malcolm led his army to another significant victory. Supported by Owen of Strathclyde, he took a great force across the border into Northumberland to meet the army of Adulf Cudel, earl of Northumbria, at Carham. Little is known about the battle, apart from the fact that the English forces were utterly defeated and countless of their men perished in the struggle. After the battle, Adulf surrendered Lothian to Malcolm, thereby extending the boundary of Malcolm's rule in the southeast as far as the River Tweed. Later in the same year, Owen of Strathclyde died. Strathclyde, which at that time included Cumbria, was placed in the guardianship of Duncan, Malcolm's grandson, thereby linking it more closely to the rest of Scotland. By 1034, when Malcolm died, the territory once known as Alba, now becoming known as Scotland, had been considerably extended.

BATTLE OF PITGAVENEY, 1040

Duncan I

Malcolm II died in 1034 and was succeeded by his grandson, Duncan. The reign of Duncan I was a short one. As was so common in the days when succession to the throne was determined by the laws of tanistry and there was more than one possible claimant, Duncan's right to be king was disputed, in particular by Macbeth, mormaer of Moray and great-grandson of Kenneth III. Much of Duncan's reign was taken up with attempts to eliminate those who contested his position as king. Twice Duncan tried to wrest power from Thorfinn, earl of Orkney and Shetland and mormaer of Caithness. Twice he was defeated, with heavy losses. The attacks on Thorfinn lost him both money and support. Duncan's activities to the south of his kingdom caused further discontent among his subjects. In 1039, he took an army into Northumberland and besieged Durham for two weeks, but Siward of Northumberland retaliated by attacking the Scots with a large force, driving them into retreat and inflicting massive casualties.

The battle of Pitgaveney

After the failure of the campaign at Durham, Duncan became aware that an alliance was forming between the mormaers of the north against him. In 1040, hoping to eliminate the central figures in the alliance, Macbeth and Thorfinn, Duncan gathered a force several thousand strong and marched northwards into Moray. He split his army to fight on two separate fronts, at Burghead and at Spynie. The division at Burghead, led by Duncan, was defeated by Thorfinn's army after a bloody battle and driven into retreat. The survivors moved towards Elgin, hoping to join forces with the rest of the body at Spynie. But Macbeth, who had successfully held back the attack on the second front, moved in to intercept Duncan at Pitgaveney. Duncan had a larger army to support him, but Macbeth's men confused them with a surprise attack. Duncan was slain in the battle – possibly by Macbeth himself – and his disheartened followers gave up the fight. Macbeth was elected king of Scotland. Duncan's two sons, Malcolm and Donald Ban, fled south, and found refuge in Northumberland.

Battle of Lumphanan, 1057

Macbeth

Most of Macbeth's reign is believed to have been a comparatively peaceful and successful time for Scotland. His position as king was undisputed for several years, until 1054, when Siward of Northumberland invaded Scotland on behalf of Duncan's son, Malcolm. Macbeth's forces were unable to prevent the loss of first Lothian and then Strathclyde to Malcolm. Macbeth's sphere of power had shrunk, but he was still not defeated.

The battle of Lumphanan

In 1057, Malcolm took up arms against Macbeth and launched an attack on the northern territories still in the Scottish king's possession. He marched his army up to Deeside, to meet Macbeth in battle. The clash took place at Lumphanan and there, either in the course of the battle or in a duel between the two men, Macbeth was slain by Malcolm. Macbeth's stepson, Lulach, was crowned king at Scone, but he was killed only months later in battle against Malcolm at Eassie. Malcolm was crowned Malcolm III, king of Scots, in 1058.

BATTLE OF ALNWICK, 1093

Malcolm III

Malcolm III (Canmore) was married twice, first to Ingiborg, the widow of Thorfinn of Orkney, and then in 1068 to Margaret, granddaughter of Aethelred of England, who had sought refuge in Scotland with her brother Edgar Atheling after the conquest of England by William of Normandy. Malcolm's marriage to Margaret brought profound cultural changes. Under Margaret's influence, both Church and court life were reformed. English fugitives from the Norman invasions were welcomed at the Scottish court by Margaret.

The alliance with England brought about by the marriage also set Malcolm against the new Norman king. Partly to harass William I, and partly in continuation of the many long years of territorial disputes that were his inheritance as king of Scots, Malcolm embarked upon the first of a series of raids into northern England in 1070. William I's response was to mount a retaliatory raid into Scotland, reaching Abernethy, where he forced a peace with Malcolm and Malcolm gave him Duncan (his son by Ingiborg) as a hostage. Nine years later, Malcolm invaded England once more and advanced as far as the River Tyne, where Newcastle now stands. He was forced back by Robert, the son of William I, and Robert then ordered the construction of the castle as a hindrance to further attacks.

In 1091, Malcolm took his men south once again and reached Durham, causing devastation as he went. In 1092,

William Rufus, son of William I, responded by marching north, capturing Carlisle and depriving Malcolm of his territory in Cumbria. There was hope that Malcolm might have the captured lands restored to him and, in 1093, he travelled to Gloucester to meet with William Rufus. He was not granted an audience, and returned to Scotland to gather an army to seek his revenge.

The battle of Alnwick

Malcolm's army advanced to Alnwick, to lay siege to the castle there. The governor of Bamburgh Castle, Robert de Mowbray, came out to meet Malcolm's force and although he had only a small body of men with him, he confused the Scots with a surprise attack. In the ensuing battle, Malcolm was killed and his followers, demoralised by the death of their king, were heavily defeated. Cumbria was still in English hands.

Battle of the Standard,
22 August 1138

1093–1124: Donald Ban, Duncan II, Edgar, Alexander

Following the death of Malcolm III, there was dispute over the succession to the Scottish throne. Malcolm and Margaret had had three sons – Edgar, Alexander, and David, but it would be four years before any of them became king. According to the laws of tanistry, Donald Ban, Malcolm's brother, was rightful successor and when Malcolm died, he brought a body of men to Edinburgh and staked his claim. The English courtiers, including members of Margaret's family, were driven from the Scottish court.

But Donald Ban's reign was to be very short. Duncan, Malcolm's son by Ingiborg, who had remained at the English court since his father handed him over as a hostage in 1070, sought help from William Rufus, the English king, to claim the Scottish throne for himself. William supplied him with an army of English and Normans in exchange for an oath of fealty, and Duncan drove Donald Ban from the throne in 1094. Duncan was murdered six months later, and Donald Ban resumed power. William Rufus then supplied Malcolm's son, Edgar, with an army, raised by Margaret's brother, Edgar Atheling. The army was met by a force of Scots and the matter was settled not by full-scale battle, but by pitting three knights from each army against each other. The English were victorious and Donald Ban was deposed and imprisoned. Edgar became king in 1097.

Edgar reigned for only ten years – he died in 1107. In 1098, following another Norse attack, Edgar ceded the Hebrides to the king of Norway. It became clear to him during his reign that Scotland was becoming a nation divided in two. The area to the south of the Forth was becoming increasingly anglicised, but to the north the land was still largely populated by Gaelic-speaking peoples and Norsemen. Shortly before his death, Edgar decreed that although Alexander was to succeed him as king of Scots, his other brother David should govern in the south of the country in Cumbria and Lothian.

Alexander's reign was relatively uneventful, but he continued the reforming process of the Scottish Church that had begun in the reign of his father, Malcolm, founding the bishoprics of Dunkeld and Moray. At the same time, he strove to keep the Scottish Church independent of the Church in England, resisting all attempts from the bishops in the south to claim supremacy over their northern counterparts.

Alexander died in 1124 and was succeeded by his brother David I.

David I

David I proved to be a wise and forward-thinking monarch. He had spent his youth in England, and when his sister Matilda was married to Henry of England, he had returned to the English court as an attendant of the queen. He was, in many ways, more Norman than Scots. Upon marrying his wife, the widow of a Norman baron, he became earl of Huntingdon. During Alexander's reign, when David had ruled in the south as earl of Cumbria, he had re-established the diocese of Glasgow and founded monasteries at Selkirk and Jedburgh. When he became king, he founded several more monasteries, five more bishoprics – Ross, Caithness, Dunblane, Brechin, and Aberdeen – and eight abbeys. During his reign the Scottish Church became wealthier than ever before, acquiring land, money, tax exemptions, etc. With its newfound wealth came power, and in future years when Scotland was struggling for its independence, its rulers would have cause to be grateful for the support of a wealthy and powerful clergy.

The spread of Norman influence in Scotland continued, and several Norman nobles, including John Balliol and Robert de Brus, were granted large areas of land. In the north, the Celtic nobles were able to retain their land, but they did so by royal charter and now ruled as earls, vassals of the king, rather than as mormaers.

Trade in Scotland began to flourish during David I's reign, and for the first time, Scotland acquired a coinage. Towns grew as centres for trade, and royal charters granted many of them burgh status, giving them rights to hold markets and to import and export goods. The burghs also exercised a degree of self-government. The crown benefited directly from the burghs, gaining revenue in the form of duties on the goods that were traded.

There was little trouble from the north during the reign of David I. In 1130, Angus of Moray led an army as far south as the Sidlaws, but the rebellion was successfully quelled. It was to England that David turned his attention, following the death of King Henry I in 1135.

Before his death, Henry had made prominent members of the nobility and clergy in England swear fealty to his daughter Matilda, but the barons were not true to their word and in place of Matilda, elected Stephen of Blois, grandson of William II, as king. Matilda was David I's niece, and so he took her side in the dispute, but family loyalty was not his only motivation, for he also hoped to gain Northumberland. He launched the first of a series of attacks on northern England in the winter of 1135–36, with a brutal and destructive advance to the border fortresses. Carlisle and Newcastle were among those that were captured. Stephen's army marched north to meet him in

February, peace was negotiated and all the fortresses except Carlisle were returned to the English king. In 1137, David invaded again, demanding the surrender of Northumberland. Stephen's army moved north to meet them, but the Scots army retired before a confrontation could take place, and Stephen turned back. Almost immediately, the Scots invaded again with a great force and for five months terrorised most of northern England.

The battle of the Standard

By the time of the second Scots invasion, Stephen of England had become preoccupied with events in the south of the country and was in no position to lead a force to retaliate against the destruction that was being caused by David's army. It was Thurstan, the elderly archbishop of York, who rallied support to fight against the invaders. He called an assembly of the barons of the north of England to ask for their help and they formed an allegiance to fight the Scottish army. Among the nobles who volunteered to fight for the English was the Norman baron, de Brus. He was a powerful landowner in Scotland, but he also held territories in England, and it was to England that he chose to demonstrate his loyalty. John Balliol, who also held lands in both kingdoms, also opted to fight for Stephen. The English army advanced as far as Thirsk, then sent a party to try to negotiate a peace with King David, promising the earldom of Northumberland for David's son, Prince Henry, if he would bring an end to the conflict, but the Scottish king refused.

The Scots army continued with their advance and had soon crossed the River Tees. The English moved forward to meet them and assembled on a plain approximately two miles north of the town of Northallerton. In the centre of their ranks, a ship's mast was raised, which they called their 'Standard', and to which had been attached a silver pyx containing the Host and the sacred banners of St Peter the Apostle, John of Beverley and Wilfred of Ripon. It was to be their inspiration and their rallying-point in battle.

The Scots army, led by King David and Prince Henry, was a mixed assembly of Norman knights, archers and spearmen from the south, Celtic chiefs and their warrior supporters, and wild Galwegians, who were poorly armed but possessed of a fearsome fighting spirit. The English army that they faced was a more orderly and disciplined array, composed mainly of cavalry, armoured spearmen and archers.

When they drew up in battle order on 22 August 1138, most of the English knights dismounted. Some stood in the front lines, interspersed with archers. Others were placed in the centre of the body along with the barons, who were grouped around the standard, ready to rally the mass of ordinary soldiers that surrounded them. At a short distance from the main body of the English army the rest of the knights, still mounted, were kept in reserve, along with the horses of the dismounted knights.

The Galwegians were the first to attack from the Scottish side, launching a frenzied charge against the mail-clad ranks of the dismounted knights and archers. The English front line faltered under the pressure of the charge, but held firm. The spears with which the Galwegians were armed were too light to effect much damage on the armour worn by their enemies, and as volley after volley of arrows poured down upon them, they began to fall. A second attack from the Scottish side was launched, led by the men of the Highlands and Isles, but they too were brought to a halt by the wall of armour presented by the English front line. The numbers of the dead and the dying continued to grow as Prince Henry mounted a desperate attack with the cavalry on the flank of the English army. They broke through to the rear of the English force to attack their horses and cavalry and managed to disperse the horses and scatter the knights, but their efforts were to no avail. In the centre of the battle, panic had broken out among the Scots and already many men were fleeing from the scene. King David tried to rally his followers for a renewed effort in vain. The battle was lost. The king was forced to withdraw with a body-guard of knights and retreat to Carlisle, where Prince Henry joined up with him. Many of the Scottish foot soldiers who had survived the slaughter of the battle were not strong enough to make the journey home.

It had been a terrible defeat for the Scots, and countless lives had been lost. England's victory was celebrated as a triumph of good over evil. Divine justice had been meted out to the invader. Nonetheless, David was not willing to give up his struggle for Northumberland and raids into England contin-ued. Eventually, in 1139, Stephen conceded Northumberland to Prince Henry. Northumberland remained in the possession of the Scots for the rest of David's reign.

BATTLE OF LARGS, 1263

1153–1249: The troublesome north and west and changing Anglo–Scottish relations

From the death of David I until the succession of Alexander III, three kings reigned in Scotland – Malcolm IV, nicknamed 'The Maiden' because he never married, William I, 'The Lion', and Alexander II. Malcolm's reign was characterised largely by his apparent submission to Henry II, to whom he gave up Northumberland and offered support at the siege of Toulouse, and from whom he gladly accepted assistance in quelling rebellion among the Celtic nobles. During his reign the balance of power in the west of the country shifted considerably. The Celtic chieftain, Somerled, gained control of Argyll from the Norse king, Olaf, and in 1156 forced a treaty with Olaf's successor, Godred, to take control of the Inner Hebrides. It was the beginning of the rise in power of the Lords of the Isles, who were to become a thorn in the side of many Scottish monarchs.

Malcolm's brother, the warlike William I, succeeded him in 1165. Relations with England were initially peaceful, but William was determined to regain Northumberland. When hostilities broke out between Henry II and his son, William instigated border warfare in 1173. One year later, however, he was captured at Alnwick Castle and taken as a prisoner to Normandy. In order to secure his release, he was forced by the Treaty of Falaise to pay homage to Henry for his kingdom and hand over his castles at Edinburgh, Berwick, and Roxburgh.

The humiliation lasted until 1189, when Richard I was on the English throne and William was finally able to regain the independence of his kingdom in return for money to support Richard in the Third Crusade. Future kings of England, however, would be less willing than Richard had been to accept that they were not the feudal superiors of the Scottish kings.

William's reign was also marked for unrest in Galloway and in the north. In Galloway, rebellion against the Norman barons and disputes over leadership troubled the area for more than 20 years and were only brought to a close when William granted the province to Roland of Galloway. The trouble in the north began in 1179 with a rebellion in favour of Donald Ban MacWilliam, grandson of Duncan II, who occupied Ross and Moray. The rebellion was quelled with the help of Roland of Galloway. In 1196, William had to return to Moray, to drive out Harold of Orkney and he had to make further excursions to the north in 1212 to quell an uprising by Guthred, son of Donald Ban MacWilliam.

Alexander II came to the throne after William's death in 1214. His reign, like that of his two predecessors, was marked by power struggles in the north, in the west and in Galloway. Early in Alexander's reign, Donald, son of Donald Ban MacWilliam, invaded Moray, but was killed by supporters of the king. An invasion by the king's army in 1222 successfully subdued the descendants of Somerled in Argyll, and a rebellion in Caithness was swiftly quelled. Galloway had been relatively quiet for a number of years, but, in 1234, Alan, Lord of Galloway died, and rebellion broke out when the province was divided between his three daughters, each of whom had married a Norman noble. Alexander managed to subdue the rebellion with the help of the earl of Ross.

Relations with England were precarious in the early years of Alexander's reign. When rebellious barons in the south appealed to Alexander for help against King John, Alexander complied. He invaded England twice – in 1216 and 1217 – and despoiled the regions of the north. Then later in 1217, he led an army down to the south of England and paid homage to Louis, dauphin of France, who had landed at Dover. As he returned to Scotland, John of England died. In 1221, Alexander married Joanna, sister of John's successor, Henry III, and relations between the two countries, although not entirely harmonious, settled. Following the death of Joanna in 1238, Alexander married a Frenchwoman – Marie, daughter of the count of Coucy – and within a few years, Scotland and England were on the brink of war once again. When Alexander refused to pay homage to Henry in 1244, both sides prepared for battle, but a peace was made on Alexander's terms, which Henry accepted.

By the time of his death in 1249, Alexander had achieved a greater degree of internal stability for his kingdom and had also secured a peace with England that was to last for 50 years. The only threat to his country's stability that he had not been able to deal with came from the Norsemen. Having failed to persuade King Haakon to sell the Western Isles, he was resolved to take them by force, but after assembling a fleet and sailing to the west coast, he fell ill on the island of Kerrara and died.

Alexander III: the threat of the Norsemen

King Alexander III was crowned at the age of eight, but did not begin ruling in his own right until 1258, when he was 17. In his minority, two powerful factions – the Comyns, supported by Balliol, and the Durwards, supported by Henry III – struggled for dominance over the young king. In 1251, Alexander was married to Margaret, daughter of Henry III, but he skilfully avoided agreeing to pay homage to Henry for his kingdom, paying homage only for his titles and possessions in England. He showed equal determination when, after the death of Walter Comyn, he began to rule in his own right and successfully kept the ambitions of his nobles in check. There was only one threat to the security of his kingdom during his reign, and that came from Norway. Kintyre and the whole of the Western Isles were under Norwegian rule. Alexander II had died before he could take them and now it was Alexander III's turn to try to claim the islands for Scotland. As his father had done, Alexander III tried diplomacy first, but was unsuccessful. Following an attack against the Norsemen on the Isle of Skye, it became clear that Haakon would be taking some form of action against the rebellious Scots to secure his dominion over the Isles, and Alexander would be forced to deal with it.

The battle of Largs

In 1263, Haakon gathered a great fleet of more than 100 ships and set sail for the west coast of Scotland. The fleet anchored between the Isle of Arran and the mainland. Alexander did not send out a force to meet Haakon but deployed defensive tactics instead, arming a line of castles close to the coast in readiness for conflict while he delayed the Norwegian king's offensive with debate. By September, Haakon was becoming convinced that nothing would be achieved by negotiation. Meanwhile, supplies were running low and the weather was getting bad – Alexander cannot have been unaware of this as he spun out the debate – and if the Norwegians did not act now, they would be forced to return to Norway with the matter unresolved.

Losing patience with fruitless discussion, Haakon sent around 50 of his ships to Loch Long, from there to cross overland (with the men dragging the ships as they went) to Loch Lomond. This force wreaked devastation on the province of Lennox, without much opposition, but the October gales set in as they made their way back to the coast, and when they set out to sea ten of their boats were destroyed in a storm. The remainder of the fleet, still waiting close to Arran, was similarly buffeted by the winds, and a number of the ships were driven ashore at Largs. When the storm had finally died down a little, Haakon and several hundred of his men landed to see what could be salvaged from the grounded ships, and Alexander advanced towards them, leading an army of cavalry and infantry. Haakon was persuaded to return to his ship while his men remained ashore to fight. There was little chance of help coming in time from the ships offshore, and his men were outnumbered by the Scots. They fought bravely as long as they could, until finally they took the chance to retreat to the sea behind them. They leapt aboard their boats and struggled out into the churning waters to rejoin the rest of the fleet.

It was hardly a great victory for the Scots, who had suffered heavy casualties with little to show for it. The Norse fleet sailed away, but their attempts to settle the dispute had been foiled not so much by the battle as by the long wait before it, which had left them short of supplies, and struggling against dangerous sailing conditions. It was Alexander's cunning and patience in postponing the conflict, rather than his skills as a military leader, that had saved Scotland from a much greater battle, and potential disaster.

King Haakon did not give up his claim to Kintyre and the Western Isles, but he died only a few months after the battle of Largs, and Magnus, his successor, reached a settlement – the Treaty of Perth – with Alexander in 1266. In exchange for an annual payment to the king of Norway, the king of Scotland was allowed to rule the Western Isles and the Isle of Man. In 1281, the relationship between the two countries was further improved when Alexander's daughter, Margaret, married Eric II of Norway.

PART II:
THE WARS OF INDEPENDENCE

Battle of Stirling Bridge, 11 September 1297

Edward I and Balliol

On the night of 19 March 1286, Alexander III of Scotland was riding to meet his second wife, Yolande de Dreux, at Kinghorn in Fife when his horse missed its footing and he fell to his death at the foot of the cliffs. Alexander's death sparked off a series of events that was to stain Scotland's soil with the blood of hundreds of men in the coming years.

Alexander and his first wife, Margaret of Norway, had had three children, but all three had died before their parents. He had only been married to his second wife for a matter of a few months. Alexander's only successor was his grandchild, Margaret, the 'Maid of Norway', daughter of Eric II of Norway and Alexander's daughter. Guardians were appointed to rule the country until the child came of age. Edward I of England, anxious to extend his sphere of control in the British Isles, managed to secure an agreement with the Scots leaders that Margaret be married to his son, Edward of Caernarvon. Arrangements were put in place for the Maid of Norway to be brought to Britain, but unfortunately she fell ill on the voyage from Norway in 1290 and died in Orkney.

There was now no direct heir to the throne, but there was no shortage of claimants. Thirteen men came forward protesting their right to become king, and unless some way could be found to settle the dispute between them, the stability of the country was seriously under threat. Two men had stronger claims than others – John Balliol and Robert de Bruce VI. Edward, having established his feudal superiority over the Scottish throne and received assurances from all 13 claimants that they were willing to accept English sovereignty over Scotland, was given the choice as to who should succeed. He chose John Balliol. In 1292, Balliol was crowned, but his reign was to be a short one. Edward's intention was to use Balliol as a puppet king under his control, and for three years he succeeded, but Balliol's patience wore thin when Edward demanded Scottish military support for his campaign against France in Gascony. Balliol refused Edward's demand and added insult to injury by entering into an alliance with the French. Edward's response was swift and savage. He stormed into Scotland in 1296, devastated the town of Berwick in an orgy of indiscriminate killing and captured the castle, then sent another army to capture Dunbar. Then he marched triumphantly to Brechin, where he demanded and secured Balliol's abdication.

The Stone of Destiny was removed from Scone and taken to England, as were the historical records of Scotland, St Margaret's black rood and the king's regalia. Three Scottish earls had been captured at Dunbar, and were taken to London. No others resisted Edward. He obtained written vows of loyalty from almost every man of any importance in Scotland. Before he departed for England, he placed the government of Scotland in the hands of his own appointed officials. A claim for the throne by Robert de Bruce VII, supported by a promise of loyalty to the English king, was ignored. Edward had no intentions of letting another king occupy Scotland's throne.

The battle of Stirling Bridge

It was not long before simmering resentment against Edward's actions turned to open rebellion. The man who sparked off this rebellion was a supporter of Balliol. He was William

Wallace of Elderslie, the son of a Scottish nobleman of minor status. He had not sworn loyalty to the English king, and was effectively living as an outlaw. He was involved in a number of skirmishes with English troops in Scotland between 1290 and 1296, and, in 1297, killed the sheriff of Lanark and burned the town. Wallace's actions encouraged others, including James the Steward and Robert Bruce, earl of Carrick, the grandson of Robert Bruce VI, to join in the revolt against the English occupiers. And while Wallace waged a campaign of guerrilla warfare in central Scotland, another man, Andrew de Moray, had also raised a force against the English in the north.

In the summer of 1297, Wallace and de Moray joined forces. Edward I was engaged in another dispute with France and could do nothing to suppress the revolt in Scotland himself. But John de Warrenne, earl of Surrey, Edward's appointed regent in Scotland, and Sir Hugh Cressingham, the lord treasurer, had gathered an army and were marching towards Stirling. Wallace and de Moray led their troops to meet them and, on 11 September, the two armies came face to face across the River Forth, Wallace's men on the north bank, the English on the south.

Between the two armies was a narrow wooden bridge, which had to be crossed before battle could commence. The English forces outnumbered the Scots five to one. The English also had cavalry, which the Scots did not. John de Warrenne hesitated at first, for although his force was superior, the crossing of the bridge would be a laborious business. Few men could cross at any one time and an army of several thousand would take a long time to reach the other side. His force would be vulnerable while split between the two banks. Wallace kept his men drawn up in battle formation on the Abbey Craig, waiting.

Finally, de Warrenne gave the order for his men to make the crossing. Wallace waited until almost half of the English force was across and then gave his men the order to attack. A large body of Scots charged down the hill to meet the oncoming English cavalry. Another detachment, under de Moray's leadership, moved between the English on the north side and the bridge, dividing the English army, blocking the way for further troops crossing, and cutting off the means of retreat for those who had crossed. Wallace had organised his spearmen into schiltrons, tightly packed circles of men protected by their shields, their long spears pointing out from the centre. These little fighting units were very difficult to break up, and they proved lethal to infantry and cavalry alike.

Panic broke out in the English ranks. The force on the north bank was the first to give way, and although the remainder on the south bank made a valiant attempt to storm the bridge, their efforts were thwarted by the seething mass of men, attacking Scots and retreating English, that barred their path. Men and horses, wounded and dying, fell from both sides into the water as the Scots continued with the slaughter. The bridge gave way under the weight of the flailing mass, and collapsed into the river. The surviving English troops, including de Warrenne, were driven into flight. Cressingham was killed in the battle. Andrew de Moray was mortally wounded in the fight and died shortly after. De Moray's death was the only dark spot in Wallace's shining victory.

Wallace was appointed guardian of Scotland. He continued his campaign southward to Berwick and soon claimed the liberation of all of Scotland. But he knew that it would not be long before Edward I retaliated. Among the ranks of the Scottish nobility, there were still many who were loyal to the English king. Wallace had to take time to recruit and train a body of men who would be capable of maintaining the struggle for his country's independence.

Battle of Falkirk, 22 July 1298

The defeat of Stirling Bridge had shaken the confidence of the English king, but Edward I was determined not to let Scotland slip from his grasp. He hastily brought matters to a close in France and returned to England to organise an army. He mustered a force of several thousand infantry and horsemen and marched north over the border into Scotland. They set up a camp to the south of the River Forth, at Kirkliston, to await the arrival of supplies that were coming by ship. Wallace, hearing of the advance, made use of this time to assemble his own troops in preparation for the inevitable encounter. He gathered them all together near Falkirk. It was a sizable army, but it was still substantially inferior to that of the English king.

Edward had intended waiting for supplies before moving on, but the supply ships had been delayed by bad weather, and now he learned that Wallace's army was not many miles away. Without taking the time to pack up his encampment, he ordered his men to march on. They spent the night just outside Linlithgow, with neither tents nor adequate food for their comfort, and moved on towards Falkirk at daybreak. The two armies faced each other on opposite slopes, with marshy ground between them. Edward's army was divided into three divisions. The first was led by Bigod, earl of Norfolk and chief marshal, and the earls of Hereford and Lincoln, the second by Sir Ralph Bisset and the bishop of Durham, and the third by Edward.

Leading the Scots along with Wallace were John Comyn of Badenoch and John Stewart of Bonkill, brother of James the Steward. There are differing accounts as to what happened and who was involved, but it is said that some sort of dispute had arisen amongst them as to who was entitled to assume supreme control over the Scottish army, and that this contributed, at least in part, to Scotland's defeat. According to some accounts, John Comyn, as a claimant for the throne of Scotland, was incensed when his desire to take command was contested. Other accounts suggest that he might have been influenced by Edward. Whatever did happen, it is almost definite that the Scots army was not operating as a united fighting force when the English made their assault. When the battle had reached a crucial stage, the Scots cavalry, with Comyn in charge, turned and left the field, leaving the Scots army sorely diminished in strength and versatility.

The first wave of attack was made by the English cavalry, and although they were initially hindered by the boggy ground that lay between them and the Scots, they did not take long to negotiate their way round it. They were successful in killing most of the Scots archers, but lost many horses and men struggling against the schiltron formations of the Scots spearmen. Then the longbowmen on the English side were called into play, and gradually, their arrows began to hit home between the ranks of shields and spears. The remaining Scots fought bravely, but without horsemen to back them up, the pressure of the English attack was becoming too much for them. As the schiltron formations began to disintegrate, Edward sent in more cavalry to finish them off, coming at them again and again until there were more bodies lying on the field than standing. Thousands of Scots were slain and William Wallace, seeing that there was no point in further resistance and bloodshed, was forced to flee to nearby woods.

Edward had reclaimed the southeast of Scotland and Wallace had lost his position as guardian of Scotland. In his place, William Lamberton, the bishop of St Andrews, Robert Bruce and John Comyn were appointed guardians. In the following years, Edward gradually re-established himself in the rest of the country, crossing the border several times to secure all the major Scottish strongholds and persuading the Scots nobility to renew their oaths of loyalty.

After travelling to France and Italy in a fruitless attempt to drum up support for the Scottish cause, William Wallace returned to England and resumed his guerrilla warfare tactics. He remained a significant thorn in Edward's side for the next few years, but he never got the chance to avenge the losses suffered by his countrymen at Falkirk. In 1305, he was betrayed to the English troops, taken to London and after a brief trial, was hanged, drawn, and quartered.

BATTLE OF METHVEN, 19 JUNE 1306

The struggle under Robert the Bruce

Robert the Bruce, grandson of Balliol's competitor for the Scottish throne in 1292, had not been a committed follower of the cause of Scottish independence. Along with his father, who served under Edward for many years as governor of Carlisle, he had been among the Scottish nobles who had pledged allegiance to Edward I after the storming of Berwick and had signed the 'Ragman's Roll'. The next year, he had taken part in the rebellion against Edward, but only briefly, surrendering to the English king after a battle at Irvine. His guardianship of Scotland did not last long, and in 1302 he gave in to Edward again and was made sheriff of Lanark. He then helped the English king to secure the surrender of Stirling Castle in 1303.

At this point, Bruce's ambitions were different from those of William Wallace; they lay not so much in securing the independence of his land as in claiming the throne for himself. In this, he sought the support of Bishop Lamberton and John Comyn. A pact was made with Lamberton and Bruce arranged to meet with Comyn to discuss the question. In 1306, Bruce and Comyn met in the church of the Minorite friars at Dumfries, but the discussion between them did not go well and soon developed into a heated argument. Bruce lost his temper and stabbed Comyn, wounding him fatally. When news of the murder reached the higher echelons of the Roman

Catholic Church, Bruce was excommunicated. With this one act of folly, Bruce had brought down the wrath of the Church and the king of England upon himself, made enemies of all Comyn's numerous supporters, and had also committed himself irrevocably to his cause.

Although Bruce had enemies, he also had supporters – including many members of the Scottish clergy, who remained committed to him in spite of his excommunication. There was no need for further negotiations, for with Comyn dead, there was no one in Scotland standing between Bruce and the throne. Within weeks of murdering Comyn, Bruce was crowned in a makeshift ceremony in the churchyard at Scone. Three months later, Edward's response came in the shape of a force led by Aymer de Valence, earl of Pembroke.

The battle of Methven

De Valence arrived in Scotland with an army of around 3000, determined to wipe out Robert the Bruce and all those who followed him. Soon Perth was in the hands of English troops. Bruce had gathered a sizable force himself and was prepared to challenge the English army in battle. But as his men camped out in the woods at Methven, to the west of Perth, de Valence's men pounced on them in a surprise attack. The Scots army, taken unawares, had no time to defend itself adequately. A vicious fight ensued, but the Scots, no matter how bravely they fought, could not recover from being caught at a disadvantage. Bruce escaped with only a few hundred followers. Seeking refuge in Argyll, they found themselves facing another hostile force, kinsmen and supporters of the murdered Comyn, and once again were lucky to escape with their lives. Scotland was full of Bruce's enemies, and Edward was moving north again. Bruce was obliged to quit the country, in the meantime at least, and went to Rathlin Island, off the north coast of Ireland.

During Bruce's absence, a number of his supporters and relatives in Scotland were captured. Three of his brothers and some other men were put to death. His sister, wife, and daughter were imprisoned. It is more than likely that news of these events would have made Bruce even more determined to win the throne of Scotland, but in addition to this it seems that in spite of his wavering loyalties in the past, the difficult and dangerous position that he had found himself in since the death of John Comyn had awakened his patriotism. The history of his struggle for Scotland's independence after his coronation is the story of a man of great courage, with inspired leadership qualities, who fought not for his own ambitions, but for his country's freedom. He returned to Scotland early in 1307 and was forced immediately into a life on the run. But slowly things began to turn his way. An ambush on a force led by Aymer de Valence at Glen Trool gave him his first victory, albeit a small one. Then in the month of May, de Valence made contact with him and challenged him to battle. Bruce must have been aware of the risks he would be taking against a better-equipped and more numerous force, but he accepted them.

BATTLE OF LOUDON HILL,
10 MAY 1307

Bruce's victory at Loudon Hill was a victory of tactics over force. De Valence had a strong force of cavalry, supported by archers. Bruce had far fewer men, no horses, and no archers. He chose a position on flat ground at the foot of Loudon Hill, on either side of which lay stretches of boggy ground. The bogs offered his small force protection from attacks on their flanks. He ordered his men to dig a row of three great ditches in front of them to protect them from a full frontal assault. The spaces between the ditches were narrow enough to be well defended by Bruce's spearmen. When de Valence drew his men up ready for battle, he was unaware of the existence of the ditches and issued the order for a headlong charge. Men and horses rushed forward to a fanfare of trumpets, ready for a quick kill, and were too late to notice the ditches. Trying to find a way between the ditches was impossible, for the wall of Scottish spears between them seemed impenetrable. Going around was equally difficult, because of the bogs on either side. The English forces were thrown into confusion, each man going this way or that without leadership or resolution. Bruce saw the chaos and chose his moment. He gave the order to charge and his spearmen moved in. The English forces had no time to reorganise themselves and were quite rapidly driven off by the Scots.

BATTLE OF BANNOCKBURN,
24 JUNE 1314

From Loudon Hill to Bannockburn

Loudon Hill was the first real blow struck by the new king of Scots against the English. The English position was further weakened by the death of Edward I in July of the same year, and the succession of his son, Edward II. Edward II had not inherited his father's skill in military matters or affairs of state. He soon became caught up in disputes with the English nobility and had neither the time nor the will to attend properly to the state of affairs north of the border. The occupying forces in Scotland were left without strong leadership and their garrisons were left short of supplies and men. England's grip on Scotland was beginning to weaken. Bruce could afford to turn his attentions away from his English enemies for a short while, and concentrate on quelling his opponents in Scotland. If he could do this and unite the Scots against the English, he stood a much better chance of success.

In the winter of 1307, he managed to crush the forces of the earl of Buchan and laid waste to his lands. In 1308, he drove Alexander of Argyll and John of Lorne out of Argyll. Bruce's brother, Edward Bruce, and his ally, James Douglas, were also working hard on his behalf. Douglas captured Thomas Randolf, Bruce's nephew who had joined the English side, and persuaded him to turn his military skills to better use fighting for his uncle. Edward Bruce captured a number of castles in Galloway. The Scottish king now had control over a large part of his country, and now felt confident enough to call a parliament in St Andrews in 1309, at which it was recognised that he, rather than Balliol, was the rightful sovereign. An attempt by Edward II to invade Scotland in 1310 proved futile, as Bruce would not be drawn into battle with him. In the next two years, Bruce's forces carried out a number of raids in the north of England, extracting large payments from the inhabitants in return for peace.

Gradually more of Scotland's strongholds fell out of English hands. An assault on Berwick was unsuccessful, but Perth was taken, then Dumfries. After having captured Dundee Castle early in 1313, it was Edward Bruce's task to secure Stirling Castle for his brother, but he soon tired of the siege. In June 1313, he made an agreement with the governor of the castle that the castle would be surrendered to the Scots on condition that an English army did not come to relieve it before midsummer 1314. It was a very rash move on Edward Bruce's part, and one that might have cost the Scots their cause, for now, inevitably, Robert the Bruce would be forced to confront the English king's army. Edward II had been effectively invited to battle, a situation that Bruce had successfully avoided up until this point. He had also been given a year's grace before the confrontation, which would allow him time to assemble a powerful force.

From the summer of 1313 until the late spring of 1314, the Scots continued with the task of capturing castles. Linlithgow, Roxburgh, and Edinburgh were taken in daring surprise attacks. Then preparations began to face the English at Stirling.

The battle of Bannockburn

Edward II crossed the Tweed at Berwick on 12 June with a massive army. For once, he had managed to persuade most of his recalcitrant nobles to rally to his cause. In addition to English troops, his numbers were swelled by Irish, French, and

Welsh auxiliaries. He led a force consisting of some 3000–5000 cavalry, 2000 archers and several thousand auxiliaries. The army was backed up by a considerable supply train, carrying food, drink, additional weapons, and siege equipment.

The Scots army was a large fighting force, but it was lacking in heavy cavalry and was considerably outnumbered. The Scots, however, had one major advantage over their enemies. They had strong, skilled leadership. The Scots king and his lieutenants – Edward Bruce, James Douglas, and Randolph – had already proved their courage and military and tactical skill, and had won the confidence and respect of their men. Edward II's reputation was that of a drunkard rather than an able leader, and his lieutenants had none of the skill and experience of the Scots leaders.

The English army was running short of time as it advanced towards Stirling. The cavalry rode on ahead and the infantry followed, becoming exhausted with the effort of a long, forced march in hot weather. Bruce had chosen his position carefully. He knew that the English army would follow the course of the old Roman road, crossing through the Torwood to the north-west of Falkirk before fording the Bannockburn en route for Stirling. To the left of the Roman road as it proceeded north-east towards the castle, the ground was wooded and hilly. To the right lay marshland, criss-crossed by several streams, including the Bannockburn, which meandered towards the Forth. Bruce positioned his men in the woodland to the left of the Roman road. As an extra defensive measure, he had numerous pits dug in the open ground which lay between his army and the route the English would have to take.

His army was divided into four sections, led by Douglas, Edward Bruce, Randolph, and himself. Randolph and his men were positioned near Kirkton of St Ninian's. In a line stretching in a south-southwesterly direction from Randolph's position, Edward Bruce, James Douglas, and the king had each assembled their own divisions.

As the English cavalry advanced towards the ford, Philip Mowbray, governor of Stirling Castle, rode out to meet them, urging the English king to turn away from battle. It was now midsummer's eve and the English were within three miles of the castle. The terms of the agreement made with Edward Bruce had been fulfilled, and Mowbray was convinced that the Scots would accept that Stirling Castle had now been relieved and would not be surrendered to them. But Edward II was determined to continue. Crossing the ford, he sent one party of his cavalry in an easterly direction towards the marshland, to follow a narrow bridle path winding through the marshes towards the castle. Edward's intention was to occupy the castle at the outset with this body of men. Meanwhile, the rest of his cavalry continued advancing along the route of the Roman road.

Two skirmishes took place between the two sides on the eve of the battle. Sir Henry Bohun, nephew of the duke of Hereford, was among the leaders of the English cavalry. After crossing the ford, he caught sight of the Scottish king and spurred his horse into a headlong charge. The attack was unexpected and Sir Henry was heavily armed. Bruce was ill-prepared and did not have the protective armour of his adversary, but as the English knight bore down upon him, he raised his axe. With one great blow, he felled Sir Henry. Bruce's men fell upon the English cavalry who had followed Sir Henry and forced them back towards the ford. Unaware of the defensive pits that had been dug, and overwhelmed by the ferocity of the Scots attack, the English fell into complete confusion, and were forced into an undignified retreat having lost several men.

Bruce, meanwhile, had noticed signs of movement to the northeast, and had realised that a party of English cavalry was getting dangerously close to the castle. He alerted the inattentive Randolph to the danger and Randolph and his men set off in a frantic dash to prevent them from reaching their destination. The English cavalry saw the Scottish spearmen charging towards them and hesitated for a moment. Should they continue towards the castle at all speed, or face Randolph's men? It was agreed that it would be cowardice not to face them, and they turned to charge. Randolph's men gathered in schiltron formation, ready to meet the advancing horses. More than 400 horsemen flung themselves at the ring of spears again and again, and with each charge more of them fell. James Douglas feared that eventually Randolph's men would be overcome by the prolonged assault, and he asked Bruce if he might take reinforcements to Randolph's aid. Bruce hesitated, and then agreed, but by the time Douglas's men had reached the site it was clear that Randolph's men had finally secured a victory. As night fell, the Scots already had two victories scored against Edward II.

The English king camped his depleted cavalry on the marshy ground, between the Pelstream and the River Forth, where they spent a damp and uncomfortable night. His infantry, tired and resentful after their long march, camped south of the ford across the Bannockburn and prepared themselves for battle with a night of heavy drinking. Bruce's men settled down in the woodland to the east of the Roman road. Bruce was now uncertain whether it would be better to fight or to move away. If he went into battle, he risked everything that he had been fighting for in the past nine years. If he led his men away, he would only lose Stirling Castle, and that loss was likely to be temporary. He held a council with his leaders and asked them what decision should be taken. They were resolved to go ahead with the battle. If Bruce was still uncertain after they had spoken, all doubts were swept from his mind by what happened next. A solitary figure appeared in the Scottish encampment and approached the king. He was Alexander Seton, a Scottish knight who had been serving under the English king. He had seen that the tide of events was turning in favour of the Scots and had chosen to defect to their side. He urged Bruce that now was the time for action, for if he were to confront the English the next day in battle, he would surely win.

The next morning at dawn the two armies faced each other. Edward's army huddled together, confined by the boggy conditions of the ground on their flanks and the rivers beyond that. The cavalry stood to the front. They watched in astonishment as the four divisions of the Scots infantry advancing towards them suddenly dropped to their knees in prayer. When Edward II realised that it was not a plea for mercy, but an appeal to God for strength in the coming battle, he gave the order for the vanguard, led by the earl of Gloucester, to charge. Bruce kept his own men in reserve as the three other divisions met the assault.

The English cavalry surged against the Scottish wall of spears. At once they began to suffer casualties. The earl of Gloucester and a number of other English nobles were among the dead. As more and more English bodies littered the ground, they hampered the progress of reinforcements, penned in by the lie of the land behind them, and prevented those who had gone beyond from getting back to regroup. Edward Bruce's men took the brunt of the English assault, but held firm. Douglas and Randolph moved on round the flank with their men to attack those who had not yet charged. The English archers were then called into play, but before their arrows could inflict too many casualties, Bruce sent a body of light cavalry, led by Sir Robert Keith, to disperse them. Bruce ordered the Scots archers to advance and fire on the English, then brought his own men into battle, moving in to reinforce the Scottish ranks where they seemed weakest. Edward Bruce's men pushed their opponents further and further back towards the main body of English troops. Now, the whole English army was forced back into the marshes.

At this point, Bruce gave a cry, and from behind a hill to the rear of the Scots encampment there came another body of people, shouting and waving banners. To the terrified English, it seemed as if Bruce had kept another division of soldiers in reserve, which was now descending upon them, but these people were not soldiers. They were camp followers, armed with little more than sticks, but the effect of their charge was dramatic. Terrible, bloody confusion reigned. The English struggled to fight back, but the wetlands claimed many horses and men, while others fell down the steep slopes of the Bannockburn and were drowned. Meanwhile the Scots hacked at them with pikes and axes, turning the pools and rivulets in the marshes red with blood. As the surviving English beat a retreat to the northwest, they found their progress hampered by even wetter ground. Some drowned in the Forth in their desperate bid to escape. King Edward escaped from the battle with his escort and made his way towards Stirling Castle, but Philip de Mowbray would not give him refuge. He was forced to ride to Linlithgow and then south to Dunbar, pursued all the way by Douglas and a body of Scotsmen.

After the battle, the Scots amassed a considerable amount of booty, left behind by the fleeing English troops. Although several members of the English nobility had been killed in battle, the Scots had also managed to take a number of important prisoners, who were exchanged for ransom. Bruce's wife, sister, and daughter were freed from captivity in return for the earl of Hereford, who had been captured by the Scots. The victory had effectively won Scotland for Bruce.

Edward II made no more effective attempts to challenge Bruce's position, but remained unwilling to acknowledge his kingship. Several members of the nobility who had fought on Edward's side now pledged their allegiance to Bruce, but he still had enemies in Scotland, notably the Comyns and Edward Balliol, son of John Balliol, who maintained his family's claim to the throne. The Scots mounted a series of devastating raids into Northumberland and Yorkshire, hoping to persuade the English king with force to come to the negotiating table. Berwick, which was the only major stronghold to remain in English hands, fell to the Scots in 1318. The remaining years of Bruce's reign were taken up with almost continual warring with the English on the one hand, and a persistent campaign of diplomacy to secure papal recognition of Scotland as an independent kingdom with Bruce as its king. The Declaration of Arbroath of 1320, signed by almost all of the most influential people in Scotland and supported by senior members of the Scottish clergy, constituted a clear affirmation of the Scots' belief in their right to be ruled by a king who would not subject them to the domination of England.

In 1323, a truce was made between England and Scotland, and Bruce finally received papal recognition of his kingship in 1324. In 1328, after the succession of Edward III to the English throne in 1327 had brought renewed fighting between England and Scotland, a treaty of peace between the two nations was signed at Northampton and the Scottish crown was returned. The treaty was sealed with the marriage of David, Bruce's son, to Joan, the sister of Edward III. Later in the same year, the pope finally lifted the ban of excommunication from Bruce.

Robert the Bruce had secured his kingship in effect with the battle of Bannockburn, but it had taken him 14 long years to win the acknowledgment of the Church in Rome and the English king, and a guarantee that his kingdom would remain separate from that of England.

BATTLE OF DUPPLIN MOOR, 12 AUGUST 1332

The struggle is renewed

Robert the Bruce died in 1329. His five-year-old son, David II, succeeded him and was crowned in 1331 at Scone. Almost all of Bruce's generation of leaders in the fight for independence had gone. Edward Bruce had been killed at the battle of Dundalk in 1318 and James Douglas was killed in Spain in 1330. There remained only Randolph, earl of Moray, and he was appointed guardian of Scotland. He found himself faced with growing opposition to the Treaty of Northampton, led by the disinherited nobility who had lost their estates in Scotland. Edward III also objected to the treaty and gave these men his support. Among the rebellious nobles was Edward Balliol, son of John, who made up his mind to claim the Scottish throne, and gathered an army to invade Scotland.

Randolph died in 1332 and the hastily appointed new guardian, Donald, earl of Mar, set out to meet the invaders with an army.

The battle of Dupplin Moor

The battle of Dupplin Moor shattered any confidence the Scots might have had in the security of their kingdom. The English army sailed from the Humber to the Forth. After landing, they marched directly towards Perth and camped at Forteviot, on the southern side of the River Earn. The main body of the Scots under the earl of Mar was camped at the northern side of the river, at Dupplin. Another large body of troops, led by Earl Patrick of Dunbar, was positioned only seven miles to the west of the English force, at Auchterarder, but there was no communication between Mar and Dunbar. The Scots forces outnumbered those of the English and perhaps this led them to suffer from over-confidence. When the English army crossed the river in the early hours of 12 August, the Scots were taken completely by surprise. The initial attack was made on a small division positioned some distance from the main body of the Scots and at once the earl of Moray led his men to their aid in a chaotic charge. They fought fiercely and with some success, and a complete victory might have been hoped for, as the earl of Mar had rallied his own division to join the battle. But instead of attacking the English flank, Mar led his men up behind Moray's division. The force of a huge body of men pressing at the back of Moray's division forced hundreds of men to the ground, where they were crushed underfoot. Meanwhile, the English archers rained arrows down upon the chaotic ranks of Scots. The battle was lost for the Scots, as much by their own folly as by anything else.

Having secured his victory on the battlefield, Edward Balliol moved to Perth and captured the city. At Scone, he was crowned king of Scotland by the earl of Fife and pledged allegiance to Edward III. Balliol's position was still far from safe, however. Mar had been killed at Dupplin, but the outraged Scots appointed a new guardian, Sir Andrew Murray. As soon as Balliol moved out of Perth, the city was reclaimed. Balliol's men were hunted down in the southwest of Scotland and attacked at Annan. Balliol escaped, but was forced to leave the country.

BATTLE OF HALIDON HILL,
19 JULY 1333

Scotland and England were at war again. Edward Balliol was not prepared to relinquish his claim to the Scottish throne and he had the support of a powerful patron, Edward III. In the spring of 1333, Edward and Balliol moved north once more. Balliol occupied Roxburgh and Edward proceeded to lay siege to Berwick. Sir Andrew Murray was captured at Roxburgh and the Scots were forced to find another man to lead them. They chose Sir Archibald Douglas, and he took upon himself as his first task the relief of the besieged Berwick. In an attempt to draw the English king away from the siege, he led his men towards Northumberland, burning and plundering. But the English would not be diverted, for they knew that Berwick must fall to them soon unless the Scots could relieve it. Douglas was forced to turn back to face them in battle.

Leaving a small siege force behind at Berwick Castle, the English army positioned themselves on Halidon Hill, approximately two miles to the northwest of the town. The site had been carefully chosen by Edward's military leaders. It afforded the English army a good view of the advancing Scots, but more importantly, its lower slopes were surrounded by marshland.

Archibald Douglas led a large army, and he may well have been optimistic about the forthcoming encounter as he led his men towards Berwick from Duns. From a nearby vantage point, he surveyed the English troops, and decided that rather than attempting to draw them down from their position, he would engage in a full frontal attack. Scots cavalry and infantry descended into the dip below Halidon Hill, unaware of the nature of the terrain that lay between them and the English. All too soon, it became obvious that a blunder had been made as horses and men floundered in the soggy marsh. For the English, the confused mass of bodies below presented an opportunity – and a target – not to be missed. The archers drew their longbows and began to fire. The Scots, unable to move at any speed because of the mud and the confusion, began to fall in their hundreds. Those that did manage to struggle to the lower slopes of the hill or higher had no strength to fight back and were slaughtered by the English cavalry, who swooped down upon them in a merciless charge. It was a terrible, bloody defeat, and amongst the hundreds of dead Scotsmen lay the body of Sir Archibald Douglas, fourth guardian in the reign of the young King David.

Battle of Neville's Cross, 17 October 1346

1333–1341: Edward III struggles for control

Halidon Hill had been a significant victory for the English and Balliol, but it was not enough to subdue the Scots in the long term. Immediately after the battle, Berwick fell to the English and Balliol was returned to the Scottish throne. Edward progressed through Scotland taking more of the Scottish strongholds and, in 1334, Balliol handed over a large part of southeastern Scotland to the English king. In the same year, the young David II and his queen were sent to France for safety. But Balliol's reign was little more than nominal, for although he had some allies in the country, the majority of Scots simply would not recognise him as king. And soon a dispute broke out among Balliol's supporters. Some of them changed their allegiance to the Scots and Balliol was forced to take refuge at Berwick. The struggle against the English continued. Robert the Steward and the earl of Moray drove the English from the area around the Clyde estuary, and William Douglas was putting up fierce resistance in the lands of the Borders.

In 1335, Robert the Steward and the earl of Moray became guardians of Scotland and continued to defy Edward's attempts to keep a hold of any substantial part of the country. Andrew Murray, who had been captured at Roxburgh, was released for a ransom, and, on the death of the earl of Moray, was reappointed guardian. Edward continued to press Balliol's case, rebuilding many of the castles that had been destroyed by Robert the Bruce, and filling them with English garrisons. He captured and burned Aberdeen, rebuilt and strengthened Edinburgh Castle and Stirling Castle and fortified the town of Perth, leaving Balliol to man it. Several other fortresses were refortified.

But Murray would not give in and after capturing Dunnottar, Kinneff, and Lauriston from Edward's men, he spent a winter engaging in guerrilla warfare against Balliol's supporters in Lothian, Angus, and Perthshire. At all times he avoided open warfare, but the countryside was laid waste in the wake of his struggles, causing hardship and famine to the inhabitants. In 1337, Edward became distracted by war with France and gradually the Scots regained control of their country. By 1341, they occupied most of the major strongholds once more, including Edinburgh, Stirling, Perth, and Dunbar. In the same year, David II was brought back from France. Now aged 17, he was old enough to rule in his own right, and the country seemed safe enough for his return.

David II

Scotland was in dire need of strong leadership when David II returned from France. The years of continual warring had taken a terrible toll; the land was impoverished and in disorder. The Scottish nobles, freed from the fear of English invasion for the first time in many years, began to fight amongst themselves. But the young king had none of his father's qualities as a leader and handled the disputes between his knights with neither firmness nor fairness. And soon he would lead his country to yet another disaster.

In August 1346, Philip VI of France suffered a terrible defeat at the battle of Crecy to an army led jointly by Edward III and his son. In the desperate hope that the English king might be diverted from causing further trouble in France,

Philip asked David II to take an army to attack northern England. Partly in recognition of treaty obligations to France and partly in an attempt to prove himself as a military leader, the young king agreed. His dealings with the English up until this point had amounted to no more than a number of raids into northern regions. This was the first time he had led a large force into battle.

The battle of Neville's Cross

David gathered an army of around 12,000 men and they marched south, plundering and burning as they went. Soon they were approaching Durham. In the absence of King Edward, the archbishop of York raised a force of around 5000 men and marched north to prepare to meet him. After a brief skirmish between an advance party of Scots and the English vanguard led by Neville at Sunderland Bridge, in which the Scots were beaten back, the two armies finally faced up to each other on the west side of the city.

The Scots were drawn up in three divisions, with Robert the Steward leading the men on the east flank, William Douglas on the west flank and David leading the central division. The English were also drawn up in three divisions. The archbishop of York was in charge of the west flank, Lord Percy the left, and Neville led the central body. King David gave the order for attack and William Douglas urged his men forward. The ground that they had to traverse was uneven and difficult and their progress was impeded by a deep gully. One of the Scottish knights, seeing that a large body of archers had been drawn up at the front of the enemy's ranks, asked for a force of Scottish cavalry to be sent among them, to disperse them before they could attack the advancing Scots, but he was ignored. Before long the English longbows were wreaking havoc as their deadly rain of arrows poured down upon Douglas's men. The Scots on the eastern flank led by Robert the Steward moved forward diagonally and managed to make some progress, but they had left their flank exposed. A reserve force of English cavalry swooped in on them with deadly effect. The Scottish army struggled on bravely, but first the west flank then the east began to disintegrate. As the men on their flanks retreated, the central body of the force, left exposed to attack on all sides, was helpless. Those who could, turned and fled. The triumphant English force captured King David, who had been wounded in the battle, and he was taken to London as a prisoner.

1346–1371: The coming of the Stewarts

After the battle of Neville's Cross, Edward took back the lands in southern Scotland that had been ceded to him by Balliol. Balliol, for his part, reasserted his claim to the Scottish throne, but was unable to exert any power beyond a confined region in the southwest. Robert the Steward was appointed as guardian of Scotland for the second time. The aftermath of the battle might have been worse, if Edward had not been preoccupied with affairs in France. In 1349, the pestilence that had swept through England two years earlier came to Scotland, killing almost one third of the population. Skirmishes in the border regions continued unabated, but otherwise an uneasy peace prevailed between the two nations. In response to an invasion of northern England in 1355, and the occupation of Berwick by the earl of Angus, Edward led an army north again. He reclaimed Berwick, and at Roxburgh was met by Balliol, who renounced his claim to the Scottish throne. Edward's army got as far as Edinburgh, but was forced to retreat when his provision ships were lost in a storm. It was his last invasion of Scotland.

In 1357, after protracted negotiations, David II was returned to Scotland, in exchange for an extortionate ransom of 100,000 merks, payable within ten years. The rest of David's reign was spent in subduing Scotland's unruly nobility and in restoring order to his financial affairs while reducing the size of his debt to the English king. David had two marriages, but produced no heir. In 1363, he agreed with Edward that upon his death, the Scottish crown would go either to Edward or his son Lionel. The agreement, not surprisingly, was seen as treachery by the Scottish parliament, who refused to recognise it. When David died in 1371, Robert the Steward, son of Marjorie (daughter of Robert the Bruce) and Walter the Steward, was crowned as king.

PART III:
TROUBLED TIMES – THE STEWART MONARCHS 1371–1625

BATTLE OF OTTERBURN, 5 AUGUST 1388

Robert II

Robert II, the first of the Stewart kings of Scotland, was 55 years old when he came to the throne, and proved to be a weak king. During his reign the power of certain noble families around Scotland flourished. Most notable among these families were the Douglases, descendants of Robert the Bruce's faithful ally James Douglas, who held sway over the Scottish Borders. In the north, the Lord of the Isles ruled over his lands almost as an independent king. Rivalries and bloody feuds between different families were allowed to carry on unchecked. Robert's strategy of marrying his daughters into powerful noble families in the hope of securing their loyalty backfired upon him. Rather than feeling themselves bound to fidelity by the arrangements, the leaders of these families considered that their kinship to the king placed them on an equal footing with him. Robert's own family members were no better than any other. When Alexander Stewart, Robert's son, who had been appointed justiciar of the north, was dismissed for negligence, his response was to burn the city of Elgin. Robert II had the crown, but his nobles wielded the power.

Fighting in the Borders continued, and a plan was made in 1388, without the knowledge of the king, to take an invasion force further into England. The earl of Fife, the king's second son, invaded Cumberland while the earl of Douglas advanced on the eastern side of the country. Douglas's force got as far as

Durham before turning back, laden with plunder. At Newcastle they stopped for two days, and a number of skirmishes took place between them and the English force led by Sir Henry Percy. In one of these skirmishes, Douglas took Percy's pennon, and declared that he would take it back to Scotland and display it from the tower of his castle at Dalkeith. Percy swore that Douglas would not get past Northumberland, and a challenge to battle had effectively been made.

The battle of Otterburn

The earl of Douglas moved his force slowly northwards. At Otterburn, they stopped and laid siege to the castle, and Douglas decided the time had come to give Percy the opportunity to reclaim his pennant. His men set up their defences, dug themselves in and waited. Their position had been carefully chosen. They placed their cattle in a dry area surrounded by marshes and barricaded them in with wagons. Their own encampment was at the foot of a small hill, which was covered with small bushes.

The Scots soldiers were resting after the toils of the day when the cry went out that the enemy was upon the camp. The Scots had been caught unawares. Most of them had taken off their armour and were now fumbling to put it back on again. Fortunately, Percy's men had not attacked the main body of Douglas's force. They had broken into the area occupied by the camp followers, who were bravely fighting them off. Hastily reassembling themselves into fighting order, Douglas's men crept out of the camp and round the hill, well concealed by the brushwood and bushes. As Percy's men continued the clash with those who still remained in the camp, they found themselves unexpectedly attacked on their flank by the main body of the Scots. Percy's men, although they fought bravely, had been thrown into confusion by Douglas's ingenious tactics. At first it looked as if they might successfully repel the Scots attack, for they had the larger force, but the Scots, with the axe-wielding Douglas in the very middle of the affray, fought with tremendous ferocity. In the midst of the battle, Douglas fell, mortally wounded. He was found by some of his knights, but he asked them to keep silent about his condition, so that his men would not lose heart. On their leader's instructions, the knights raised his banner and with a cry of 'Douglas', resumed the battle. As the English finally succumbed to the relentless battering of his men, Douglas died.

BATTLE OF THE CLANS, 1396

Robert III

In the same year as the battle of Otterburn took place, Robert II's second son, Robert Stewart, earl of Fife, was appointed guardian of Scotland, making Robert II virtually redundant as king. In 1390, Robert II died and his first-born son, John, the earl of Carrick, succeeded him, taking the name of Robert III. The earl of Fife kept his role as guardian. The new king was no stronger than his father had been. Disorder continued in the country and clan warfare in the north was getting out of control.

The battle of the clans

In an attempt to bring about a final settlement between two warring clans and bring an end to years of bloodshed, a gory spectacle was arranged at the North Inch in Perth. King Robert III, the earl of Fife (soon to become the duke of Albany), and a number of foreign dignitaries were in attendance. There is some dispute as to which two clans took part in the conflict – Clan Chattan and Clan Kay, Clan Chattan and Clan Cameron, or two warring septs of Clan Chattan, Clan Macpherson and Clan Davidson. The identities of the participants are perhaps less important than the means by which their dispute was settled. The king clearly did not have enough power over the Highland warlords to impose peace through force, sanction or diplomacy. He had sent the earl of Moray and the earl of

Crawford to try to settle the matter, but they had been unsuccessful. The solution that was hit upon was to hold a public contest, a staged fight between the two clans. Each clan was to be represented by 30 men, who would fight to the death. The North Inch was prepared as an arena for the contest, complete with barriers to keep the audience at bay and seating for the invited guests.

Legend has it that one man elected to fight for one side (either Chattan or Macpherson) went missing just before battle was due to commence, and that an armourer from Perth, Henry Wynd, stepped in to take his place. Fortunately, he found himself on the winning side.

The men were all armed in the same way, with a bow, a sword, a knife and an axe. Battle commenced with arrows flying through the air from both sides, then the bows were thrown aside and the combatants charged at each other to engage in brutal and bloody hand-to-hand combat. The battle was short, but it made a horrifying spectacle. At the end, Clan Chattan (or Macpherson) emerged as victors, but only ten of their men were left standing. On the other side (Kay, Davidson, or Cameron) all but one of the combatants were killed. The survivor jumped into the Tay and swam for his life.

Battle of Homildon Hill, 14 September 1402

Background to the battle

Relations between Scotland and England were still strained at the beginning of the 15th century and the feuding between the nobles, unchecked by the weak duke of Albany, governor of the kingdom, was to be instrumental in bringing about a fresh outbreak of warfare.

In 1399, Robert III's son David, the duke of Rothesay, was appointed lieutenant of the kingdom. An arrangement had been made for Rothesay to marry the daughter of the earl of March, and the king had been paid handsomely by the earl for the privilege. The arrangement foundered when the earl of Douglas made a higher offer for his daughter to marry the young duke. Rothesay married Douglas's daughter and the earl of March demanded his money back, without success. March went to England where he was treated sympathetically by Henry IV, and in his absence the Douglases took possession of his castle at Dunbar. He demanded that it should be restored to him but was refused, and hostilities between Scotland and England broke out again. March brought a mixed force of English and Scots north to claim back his fortress, but was driven back by the Douglases. In 1400, Henry IV brought an army into Scotland, but was forced to withdraw before a battle was fought. Then in 1402, Archibald, the fourth earl of Douglas, led an invading army across the border.

The battle of Homildon Hill

The Scots, led by Douglas, were close to Newcastle when they learned that an army led by the earl of March and Sir Henry Percy, commonly known as Hotspur, was advancing to meet them in battle. The Scots gathered in a tight body on Homildon Hill, ready to face the enemy. Hotspur, true to his hot-headed nature, was ready to take on the Scots in a headlong charge, but the earl of March, seeing the compact mass of the Scots before him, advised against it and brought forward the archers. In the Scottish ranks, meanwhile, a repeat of the battle of Neville's Cross was being played out. One of the Scottish knights implored his leader to send the cavalry out to disperse the ranks of English archers before they could begin firing. He rallied a small number of horsemen around him for the charge, but the move was made too late and the numbers were too small and they were easily picked off by the English bowmen. The rest of the Scottish army made a standing target for the archers' arrows, and most were slain before having made any sort of advance. There was no close combat, and little retaliation from the Scots. The result was a humiliating defeat after which several Scottish prisoners were taken, including Murdoch Stewart, son of the duke of Albany.

The battle was the last major encounter with the English in Robert III's lifetime.

BATTLE OF HARLAW, 24 JULY 1411

The captive king

Robert III died in 1406. His eldest son, David, the duke of
Rothesay, a wild and impetuous young man, had died in 1401,
after being imprisoned in Falkland Palace by the duke of Albany.
Feeling anxious for the safety of his other son, James, Robert
had arranged for him to travel to France, but shortly after Prince
James, then aged eleven, had been picked up by a French ship it
was captured by the English. James was taken as prisoner to England. On the same day, 4 April, his father died. In the absence
of the young king, the duke of Albany was appointed governor
of the kingdom, but he ruled more by submitting to the will of
his nobles than by imposing his own will upon them.

The battle of Harlaw

In the Highlands, the people were a law unto themselves. Until
this point the Highlanders had been preoccupied with conflicts
among themselves and had not posed any threat to the people
of the Lowlands, but the power of Donald Macdonald, Lord of
the Isles, had been steadily increasing. He had control of the
Hebrides and the western Highlands. Now he wanted to
extend his realm to include the earldom of Ross, to which he
believed he had a claim through marriage. The duke of Albany,
on the other hand, felt that it should belong to his son, John,
earl of Buchan.

Macdonald led several thousand men eastward in pursuit of his claim, and was met at Harlaw near Aberdeen, by Alexander Stewart, the earl of Mar, with an army he had gathered from the locality, in particular from Aberdeen itself. The battle that ensued was long and fierce, with great losses on both sides. In the end, the greater loss of men was from the earl of Mar's army, but they refused to give in and at length the Lord of the Isles led his men away, having neither suffered a defeat nor secured a clear victory. The northeast of Scotland, however, remained beyond the bounds of his control.

Battle of Baugé, Easter Eve, 1421

James I was still in captivity in England when France made an appeal to the Scots for help. Following his victory at the battle of Agincourt, Henry V of England had taken possession of Normandy and his allies held Paris. The English army under Henry's brother, the duke of Clarence, now looked set to continue southward, to take Orleans and Tours. The Scots rallied to the support of the French, and an army of around 7000 men arrived in France in 1421 under the leadership of the earl of Buchan.

The Scots travelled to Baugé, where the duke of Clarence and his army were holding the castle under siege. It was Easter time and the two armies agreed that a truce should be made, with no fighting between Good Friday and Easter Monday. The English army withdrew to Beaufort and the Scots set up an encampment close to Baugé. The Scots army was taking its ease on the day before Easter Sunday when the alarm was sounded. The English army had broken the truce and was about to seize the bridge at Baugé. The Scots hurriedly sent an advance party of around 100 men to hold the bridge while the rest of the army assembled and prepared for battle. It took some time for the English infantry to force their way past the Scots blockade, by which time the Scots were ready to attack. The English cavalry and archers were still at the other side of the river when the Scots charged. The ensuing battle was long and bloody, but resulted in a resounding victory for the Scots. The duke of Clarence was killed and several other English nobles were either killed or captured.

In 1423, the earl of Douglas brought another force over from Scotland to join those who were already in France, but sadly the triumph at Baugé was not to be repeated. A defeat at Crevant was followed by another devastating defeat the following year, at Verneuil.

Battle of Verneuil,
17 August 1424

The Scots were fighting alongside the French in this battle. There were also a number of Italian crossbowmen and cavalry in the army. The dauphin was not present at the battle. The French troops were under the command of the duc D'Aumale, but overall command of the army was given to the earl of Douglas. The English army was smaller than the Franco–Scottish force, but it was well organised. Bedford, who was in overall command, had several competent leaders in the field, including the earl of Salisbury and the earl of Suffolk.

The Scots were drawn up to the right of the French infantry in the centre of the line, with cavalry and archers on either flank. Facing them, the English army had arranged the centre of their line with dismounted knights and spearmen. Archers were positioned on the flanks. Mounted knights and another body of archers stood at the rear, close to the horses of the dismounted cavalry. As the English began their advance, French cavalry suddenly charged through the archers on one flank, but were repelled by arrows from the archers at the rear. As the fighting continued in the centre of the field, more French cavalry tried the same manoeuvre on the opposite flank, but were driven off. The French infantry troops were the first to give way in the centre of the line, while the Scots held firm. Soon, with their support on all sides driven from the field, the Scots found themselves facing the full brunt of an English assault that hemmed them in on all sides. The vast majority of the Scots were slain. At the end of the battle, around 6000 bodies littered the field. The earl of Buchan and the earl of Douglas were among the dead. It was a huge sacrifice to make and although a number of Scots were present in further battles in the Hundred Years' War, this was the last time Scotland played a major part in the struggle for France.

BATTLE OF SAUCHIEBURN,
11 JUNE 1488

1423–1460: The threat of the Scots nobles

In 1423, James I was released from his captivity in England, having promised to pay £40,000 to the English king as 'expenses'. He was married in February 1424 to Lady Joan Beaufort and that May was crowned at Scone. James was well aware that there were many rivals to his authority and almost immediately set about removing any threats from them. The earl of Lennox was executed, along with the duke of Albany and two of his sons. Several other nobles had their lands confiscated, and the king took control of the earldoms of Lennox, Buchan, Mar, Dunbar, and others. Through these measures, along with legal reforms, the power of the Scottish nobility was diminished significantly. The troublesome Highland chiefs were also treated with severity. In 1428, James held a parliament in Inverness. All the Highland chiefs were summoned, and upon their arrival, imprisoned. Some were executed, others banished. The Lord of the Isles escaped, and burned Inverness before being captured and forced to submit. James's measures brought an uneasy peace to the Highlands for a while, but it would not last.

The nobles were seething with resentment at their treatment at the hands of the king. A revolt was almost inevitable. A conspiracy was formed between the earl of Atholl, Sir Robert Stewart, and Sir Robert Graham, and, in February 1437, when James was staying at Blackfriars monastery in Perth, he was attacked and murdered.

James II was only six years old when his father was killed. Three noble figures had come to prominence in Scotland by this time – Alexander, earl of Ross and Lord of the Isles, the earl of Crawford, and the earl of Douglas. Of the three, the earl of Douglas was the most powerful. Archibald, fifth earl of Douglas, was appointed governor of the kingdom in James II's minority. Two less powerful nobles, Sir William Crichton, warden of Edinburgh Castle and Sir Alexander Livingston, governor of Stirling Castle, vied with each other for custody of the young king, while Douglas paid little attention to the government of the country and permitted lawlessness to reign unchecked. When the fifth earl of Douglas died and his son William became the sixth earl, Livingston and Crichton, who was now chancellor, put their differences aside to face the threat of the growing power of the Douglas family. In 1440, William Douglas and his brother David were invited to dine with Livingston, Crichton, and the young king at Edinburgh Castle, where they were dragged from the table and murdered.

James, the seventh earl of Douglas, died in 1443 and was succeeded by William, who tried to increase his power through intrigue. He won Livingston and the young king over and became lieutenant-governor of the kingdom. In 1452, aware that a dangerous league had formed between the earls of Douglas, Crawford, and Ross, James invited Douglas to dinner at Stirling Castle and murdered him. James, the ninth earl of Douglas, and the earl of Crawford rose against the king in rebellion, only to be defeated. But the danger from the Douglas family was not yet over. The ninth earl continued stirring up trouble in the Western Isles and south of the border. In 1455, James II advanced against the Douglases with an army. Their castles were destroyed and their lands ruined. The earl of Douglas fled to England. His three brothers held out in the Borders for some weeks, but at Arkinholm one was killed, another captured and executed, and the third forced to flee. The Douglas family were outlawed and their estates forfeited.

With the danger from the Douglas family thus removed, James II turned his attentions to the south, where the Wars of the Roses had broken out. James had real fears of an English invasion and had mounted warning beacons on the hills along the border with England as a precaution. In 1460, he was finally moved to invade England at the instigation of Henry VI, and laid siege to Roxburgh Castle. On 3 August, he was standing beside a cannon that was ready to fire on the castle. The barrel of the cannon burst, and James was killed.

James III

James III was nine years old when his father died. Roxburgh Castle succumbed to the Scottish siege not long after the death of James II and in 1461 Berwick was returned to the Scots by the Lancastrians. But the country was in a dangerous position. In the north, John of the Isles and the exiled earl of Douglas were negotiating with Edward IV of England, intent on the conquest of Scotland. Their plan was for Douglas and the Lord of the Isles to rule in the north as vassals of Edward, who would control the lands south of the Forth. The treaty between them did not result in any substantive action in the early years of James's reign, but was to remain a threat.

In 1465, Bishop Kennedy and the queen mother, Mary of Gueldres, who had led the Scots council in the king's minority, died. Through elaborate scheming, Lord Robert Boyd succeeded in establishing himself as chamberlain, while his son, Thomas, was created earl of Arran and was married to Mary, the king's older sister.

The following years were notable for the negotiations between Scotland and Denmark that resulted in the annexation of the islands to Scotland. A marriage was arranged between Margaret, daughter of Christian I of Denmark, and the young Scottish king. This arrangement wiped out Scotland's rental arrears for the Western Isles and brought with it the promise of

60,000 florins as the princess's dowry. Unable to make the full payment, Christian pledged Orkney and Shetland as security, but by 1472 he was still unable to find enough money and Orkney and Shetland were annexed to the Scottish Crown.

The arrival of the new queen of Scotland in 1469 was the signal for James to take charge of his country. Lord Robert Boyd and his son, the earl of Arran, fled into exile. Sir Alexander Boyd, Lord Boyd's brother, was executed.

James III was a weak king, and unpopular with his nobles. He preferred mental exercise to the rigours of battle and preferred to try to deal with conflict with England through pacification and marriage treaties, rather than fighting. His efforts were unsuccessful. He was finally moved to take action in 1475 when the scheming between the Lord of the Isles and Edward of England came to light. He sent an expedition to the Western Isles in 1476 and John Macdonald was brought back to Edinburgh, where he surrendered all his lands to the king. They were all returned, however, with the exception of the earldom of Ross. The king did not cultivate the company of men from Scotland's powerful families. Instead, Robert Cochrane, an architect and builder, and William Rogers, a musician, counted among his favourites, and the privileges bestowed upon them aroused deep resentment among the men of higher rank, whom James had ignored.

James cut a poor figure when compared with his two brothers, Alexander, the duke of Albany and John, the earl of Mar, and he knew that there were many people among his subjects who considered that the duke of Albany would be a more effective ruler. In 1497, both brothers were imprisoned on charges of using witchcraft against the king. The earl of Mar died – possibly murdered – but Albany made a daring escape from his prison in Edinburgh Castle, and allied himself with Edward IV. Albany had the support of a number of prominent nobles, including the earl of Angus. James was becoming increasingly isolated.

In 1481, difficulties with England increased. James was being pressurised by France to attack England and at the same time, the king of England was once again negotiating with the Lord of the Isles. An English fleet sailed up to the Forth, but was driven back. James felt bound to retaliate, and prepared for battle against England, but his support was dwindling. His discontented nobles were now plotting against him and in 1482, when James's army had reached Lauder, they took action. James's favourites, including Cochrane, whom he had made earl of Mar after his brother's death, were hanged from a bridge and James was returned to Edinburgh Castle as a prisoner. Albany led an English force into Scotland and the Scottish nobles made a truce with him. Albany remained in Scotland, but the English army, on its return across the border, captured Berwick. It was the last time that Berwick would change hands between Scotland and England.

James was released from Edinburgh Castle, but Albany saw himself as more powerful. He was appointed lieutenant-governor of the realm, a position that gave him control over military affairs. In 1483, he sought to consolidate his position in Scotland by entering into a league with Edward to help him seize the crown. His plans were discovered and he lost his position as lieutenant-governor, but his reluctance to abandon his scheming resulted in charges of treason and he was forced to flee the country. In 1484, he returned to Scotland with the exiled Lord Douglas and a modest army, but got no further than Lochmaben. Douglas was captured and Albany fled to France.

The danger from Albany was past, but James was still threatened by several other prominent nobles, who sought to better their own positions. Rather than seeking to make his peace with them, James added to his problems by attempting to turn the collegiate church of Coldingham into a chapel royal, setting the powerful Border family, the Homes, who claimed ownership of Coldingham, against him.

The king's young son, Prince James, was seen by the rebellious nobles as the key to their success. He was taken, not unwillingly, by the conspirators, and they proclaimed him governor-elect. The king was now faced with a rebellion that claimed his own son as its figurehead. The two sides gathered forces. James looked to the north for support, and led an army south across the Forth. There were outbreaks of fighting with the rebels around the castle of Blackness, then a tentative truce was made and James returned to Edinburgh. But the rebels had not disbanded, and an army, led by Prince James, was soon on the march. The king, knowing that conflict was inevitable, went to Stirling to meet up with his supporters from the north. Stirling Castle offered him no refuge: the governor favoured the rebels. James could either flee and suffer whatever humiliations followed, or face the enemy. He chose the latter and drew up his forces ready for battle just to the south of Stirling, at the Sauchieburn.

The battle of Sauchieburn

Historians differ regarding the number of men that followed the king into battle, but his army is thought to have outnumbered the rebels by several thousand. A number of prominent men counted among the leaders, including the earl of Menteith, the earl of Crawford, Lord Erskine, Lord Graham, Lord Ruthven, and Lord Maxwell. The army was drawn up in similar fashion to that of the rebels, in three divisions, the first led by Lord Home and Lord Hailes, the second by the young prince, and the third by Lord Gray. Little is known about the events of the battle itself. In the early stages, it appeared that the royalist forces had gained the advantage, but soon they were being pushed back by the rebels. The king, who had been in a state of high agitation before the battle, seemed to take fright and galloped off the field. His men continued with the battle and fought bravely for several hours without their king, but gradually they began to give way and their fighting spirits, depleted by rumours of the king's death, ebbed away to nothing. When they began the retreat towards Stirling, the rebels did not pursue them. The battle had been won and there was no need for any more senseless slaughter.

The king had gained nothing from his cowardly flight. It is thought that he was making his way to the Forth, where the loyal Admiral Wood waited with the royal fleet, but he did not get past Bannockburn. He fell from his horse outside a miller's cottage and was taken inside for his wounds to be treated. When he asked for a priest, the miller and his wife asked who he was, and he told them, 'I was your king this morning.' The miller's wife at once ran from the house, calling for a priest for the king. A man claiming to be a priest came to him, gave him the sacrament, heard his confession and then stabbed him to death with his own sword.

It is unlikely that the conspiring nobles had meant for the king to die when they took up arms against him. Forcing his abdication was one thing; being a party to his murder was an entirely different matter. Although he had been deeply unpopular with many of his nobles, a number of prominent and influential people had remained loyal to him and they were appalled by the manner of his death. The new king was distraught when he learned of the death of his father and wore an iron chain around his waist for the rest of his life as penance. The leaders of the rebellion, in particular the Homes and the Hepburns, were rewarded for the parts they had played by being given positions of power. But there was to be no action taken against those who had fought for the king. By 1490, the new king was at peace with his father's former allies.

Battle of Flodden,
9 September 1513

The reign of James IV

James IV's character contrasted strongly with that of his father. Although he was as interested in the arts and sciences as his father had been, his intellectual curiosity was not accompanied by the same aloofness. Nor did he shrink from displays of physical prowess. His love of sport and his abilities as a horseman and swordsman were well known and were frequently displayed in hunts and tournaments at which he entertained his guests lavishly. His energy and enthusiasm were obvious in all aspects of his life and, as a king, he ruled with as much passion for the fate of the common man as concern for the wider affairs of state.

James IV was 15 years old when he came to the throne. Whilst acknowledging the debt he owed to the nobles who had placed him there, he was old enough and strong enough to establish his authority as a king who was going to rule in his own right, and not as the puppet of powerful barons. The threat from the 'Black' Douglases, so long a thorn in the sides of the Scottish kings, was gone. A brief rebellion by the earl of Lennox and Lord Lyle, who felt their part in the new king's success at Sauchieburn had not been given the recognition it deserved, came to nothing. The earl of Angus, former ally of the duke of Albany, still displayed pro-English sentiments, but he too was silenced. His lands at Eskdale were forfeited. In the southern part of the country at least, James kept his nobles firmly on side.

There was still disorder in the Highlands, however. In 1493, the territories of the Lord of the Isles were forfeited to the Crown and James travelled to the Western Isles to make peace with the vassal chieftains. He returned in 1494 and fortified and garrisoned the castles of Tarbert and Dunaverty, but as soon as he departed, the garrison at Dunaverty was driven out and the governor hanged. The perpetrator, John of Isla, was captured and executed, but the unrest continued, and James had to return to the Highlands several times in 1495, 1498 and 1499. In 1500, he made the earl of Argyll lieutenant-general of the Isles and there was a short, uneasy period of peace. Then in 1504, there was another rising, in support of Donald Dubh, grandson of John of the Isles. The earl of Huntly was ordered to suppress it, and four new sheriffs were appointed to enforce law and order. The powers given to Huntly and Argyll by the king shifted the balance of power in the Highlands. The Macdonalds were now in decline, but the Gordons and the Campbells were rising to take their place. James had done more than his predecessors to suppress the lawlessness endemic in the region, but the problem was far from solved.

Relations between Scotland and England were not peaceable in the early years of James IV's reign. In 1496, James took up arms in support of Perkin Warbeck, who claimed to be the duke of York (one of the murdered 'princes in the tower'), and led a force across the border. His army gathered a healthy booty from looting and plundering in the northern counties, but found no support for Warbeck's cause in England and was obliged to return. In 1497, another Scots army invaded England, and a third offensive in 1498, in which Norham Castle was put under siege, was only brought to a halt by the threat of a larger English army marching north. In 1499, a Treaty of Perpetual Peace was signed between Scotland and England and, soon after, it was arranged that James would marry Margaret Tudor, daughter of Henry VII. The marriage took place in 1503 and there was no further conflict with England while Henry VII was alive. But the death of Henry VII and the succession of Henry VIII in 1509 brought renewed difficulties, and these, combined with affairs in the rest of Europe, would result in tragedy for James and his country.

From the earliest years of his reign, James had worked to build up the Scottish navy. A military harbour was built at Newhaven and several new ships, including the massive *Great Michael*, unsurpassed in size and firepower, were constructed. With the assistance of his two great naval commanders, Sir Andrew Wood and Andrew Barton, James had set about tackling the piracy problem in the North Sea, dealing with English, French, and Dutch pirates with equal severity. The new English king, Henry VIII, did not take kindly to the presence of Scottish ships off the coast of southern England, however. In 1511, claiming that it was the Scots who were the pirates, the English captured two Scottish ships in a sea battle in which Andrew Barton lost his life. Relations between Scotland and England were also strained on a more personal level. Henry VIII persistently refused to hand over jewels that Margaret Tudor claimed were hers by right. The 'perpetual peace' between Scotland and England was seriously threatened, and soon pressure from Europe would lead James to break it.

Pope Julius II wanted to drive the French out of their territories in Italy and wanted to secure the support of Scotland. In 1507, the pope presented James with the silver-gilt sword which remains part of Scotland's regalia, ostensibly in recognition of Scotland as a 'special daughter', but partly as a bribe to encourage James to sever links with France. James, still tied by an alliance to France, found himself caught between the two. In 1510–11, England joined the Holy League against France with Spain and Austria. The pope made an appeal to James for his assistance in Europe, but James was already becoming disillusioned with Henry VIII and his scant regard for the Treaty of Perpetual Peace with Scotland. In 1513, when the queen of France appealed to James for help, asking him to invade England, James decided that his loyalties to France took precedence over any obligation he might have towards maintaining friendly relations with Henry VIII. With the support of the majority of his nobles, he opted to side with France and declared war on England.

Now was the time when the Scottish fleet might have played a vital role for Scotland. Ships were sent out in July 1513, but instead of sailing to France to deal with the forces of Henry VIII which were already besieging Terouenne, they went to Ireland. Whether it was a deliberate tactic on James's part or the decision of the earl of Arran, who acted as admiral, is unclear. After a few minor skirmishes with the English occupying forces there, the ships returned and remained idle throughout the rest of the hostilities.

The battle of Flodden

James assembled his army for the invasion of England at the Boroughmuir, just outside Edinburgh, in August 1513. It was the largest army that had ever been gathered by a king of Scotland, and it was also the best equipped. Several cannons were sent southwards in advance of the main body of the army, which crossed the border into England on 22 August. But although the army was large, it lacked cohesion. It had been assembled from all parts of the country, Lowlands and Highlands, east and west, and it contained groups of soldiers who were unused to fighting alongside each other and whose styles of combat were different. Their leader, the king, might be honourable, bold and daring, but his skills as a military strategist had never been severely tested. These two factors would prove significant in the disaster that was to befall them. They made a promising start. Norham Castle was captured, and Etal, Wark, Ford, and Chillingham also fell. As the Scots moved south, the earl of Surrey moved north, gathering his army as he went. Most of the soldiers from the south of England were in service in France, and so Surrey drew from the resources of the northern counties to assemble his force, which is thought to have numbered around 25,000 men. A fleet under Surrey's son, Sir Thomas Hood, sailed up the coast with additional artillery, supplies, and men.

The two sides drew closer near Wooler, and a heraldic exchange took place between the two leaders. It was agreed that battle would take place on 9 September, on a site that would allow the two armies to meet on equal terms. The Scottish army assembled on a ridge on Flodden Hill, which would immediately place the English at a disadvantage if they were coming from the lower ground to the south. But the earl of Surrey made a daring decision. He took his army east across the River Till and then northwards, past the Scots army on the other side of the river. Five miles to the north, they turned again, and proceeded to recross the Till at Twizel Bridge, and head back towards the Scots. This manoeuvre placed Surrey's army between the Scots and Scotland. When he realised what was happening, James was forced to reassemble his forces in new positions, ready to face the unexpected line of attack.

Surrey's manoeuvre gave the Scots an opportunity for rapid victory. The crossing of the Twizel Bridge was slow and laborious. Had the Scots king chosen to launch an attack at this point, there is every possibility that the English army would have been devastated, but it seems that James was more intent on honourable combat than swift victory, for the opportunity was not taken. With his army deployed on a ridge at Branxton, he waited until the English had assembled on high ground a mile or so to the north.

The stormy weather and the marshy conditions on the low ground separating the two sides were going to make it a grim struggle for all concerned, whoever might emerge as victor. The Scots were arranged in five divisions. The earl of Huntly and Lord Home took charge of the Borderers on the left flank, while on the right, Argyll and Lennox took charge of the

Highland forces. James led the centre of the field, surrounded
by the finest men of the Scots army. The English faced them in
four divisions, three divisions standing in front, led by Sir
Thomas Howard, the earl of Surrey, and Sir Edward Stanley,
with Lord Dacre taking charge of a reserve force of cavalry
behind them.

Battle commenced at around four o'clock in the afternoon,
with artillery fire from both sides. The English cannon fire
did considerably more damage than that of the Scots, for the
Scots cannon were poorly positioned and offered little cover
for the infantry advancing down the slope. Early on in the
battle, the leader of the Scots artillery was killed. The two
divisions on the Scottish left advanced against the English
right. The ferocity of the Borderers' attack was initially effective, dispersing large numbers of the English infantry, but
Lord Dacre, coming in from the rear with some of his cavalry,
put the Scots to flight before they could follow up on their
advantage. The Highlanders, charging against the left wing of
the English army, were unable to break through the ranks of
pikemen drawn up to face them. In the centre, where their
gallant king was fighting with the flower of the army, the two
sides were embroiled in a grim and bloody tussle, in which it
was not clear which one had the advantage. Then Dacre
brought his cavalry round to attack the Scots from the rear
and Stanley, having successfully repelled the Highlanders'
advance, launched his men against the right flank. The Scots
were being attacked on all sides and although they fought
grimly on, their numbers dwindled with increasing speed. At
some point in the struggle, the Scots king was killed. As darkness descended the small band of survivors slipped away from
the field. The English were too exhausted to pursue them.

The losses on both sides were enormous. The English had
lost almost 5000 men. The Scots death toll was approximately
10,000, more than 20 of whom were members of the nobility.
All over Scotland, families mourned their dead. The reign of

James IV, the colourful, gallant hero of his people, had ended in tragedy. His son and heir was only 17 months old. Once more, Scotland's stability would be threatened by power-hungry nobles.

BATTLE OF SOLWAY MOSS, 24 NOVEMBER 1542

James V

Margaret Tudor, wife of James IV, was appointed regent in her son's minority, according to the wishes of her dead husband, but, in 1514, she married Archibald 'The Red' Douglas, earl of Angus, and lost her position as regent. In 1515, John Stewart, duke of Albany, son of the duke of Albany who had been exiled during the reign of James III, returned from France and was appointed in place of Margaret Tudor.

Albany's regency was troubled. Almost immediately he found himself at odds with Lord Home, the chamberlain. The earl of Angus and the earl of Arran added to his problems, competing both together against him and against each other for power. Each time Albany returned to France, trouble broke out anew. Lord Home and his brother were hanged for treason in 1516, but Argyll and Arran continued to conspire against the duke. In 1521, Albany's troubles multiplied when Henry VIII demanded his removal as regent. He returned to France to find military support against England and Henry VIII took advantage of his absence to plunder the Borders. Albany hastened to retaliate and besieged Wark Castle with French troops and Scottish Borderers, but when the weather turned foul the Borderers decided to retreat while they still could and left the French troops to their fate. Albany left for France again – this time for good.

Albany's departure left Angus free to assume primacy. Angus, who had taken charge over the young king in 1517 and had kept him virtually a prisoner, soon wormed his way to power. He persuaded parliament in 1526 that he had the king's 'royal authority'. The Douglas family virtually ruled in Scotland, with relatives and allies of the earl of Angus filling most of the prominent positions in government. The young king, from the age of 14 until he was 17, was virtually a puppet, manipulated by the earl of Angus.

At the age of 17, James V rebelled and managed to escape from Falkland Palace, where he was being kept. He rode to Stirling Castle, gathered a force of men, and proceeded to take charge of the country himself. The earl of Angus fled from Edinburgh. A few months later the Douglas lands were forfeited to the Crown. James personally drove the earl of Angus from his stronghold at Tantallon Castle. The Master of Forbes, the earl's brother-in-law, was executed and Lady Glamis, his sister, was burned for witchcraft.

In the following years, James devoted much of his energy to restoring order to the Borders and the Highlands. His methods were severe. In the Borders, he hanged more than 40 Border reivers, most notably Johnny Armstrong and members of his family. In the Highlands, a number of the troublesome chiefs were executed or imprisoned, while others were persuaded to submit to the king.

There were more serious problems building up for James V, however. The Scottish parliament was still strongly Catholic, but the influence of the Reformation in Europe had spread to Scotland and although Protestantism was denounced by parliament as heresy, the power of the Catholic Church, which James wholeheartedly supported, was under threat. In England, his uncle, Henry VIII, had converted to Protestantism and was eager for James to follow his lead. In 1534, another 'perpetual peace' had been made between Scotland and England, but Henry could not be sure of this while Scotland still clung to its old alliance with France. If James could be persuaded to convert to Protestantism, his ties with France would become weaker.

Henry sent ambassadors to Scotland to try to convert James on two occasions, but without success. James's marriages to French Catholic women did not help matters. In 1537, he married Madeleine, daughter of the French king, Francis I. She died only a few months later, and, in 1538, James married Mary, sister of the duke of Guise.

Relations between Scotland and England became increasingly strained over the next three years. As had happened so often before, trouble in the Borders escalated, as Henry goaded his nephew, forcing him to choose between Protestantism and war with England. In 1542, an English fleet attacked Scottish merchant ships off the coast of Scotland and later in the same year, Sir Robert Bowes led a sizable army across the border, which fortunately was repelled. Another raid resulted in the burning of Kelso before the English army retreated. James was already losing strength from the disease that would ultimately kill him. He tried to persuade his nobles to launch a counter-invasion of England, but the memory of the disaster at Flodden had left them reluctant to do this. Nonetheless, a considerable Scottish army was raised in the autumn of 1542 and advanced towards the border.

The battle of Solway Moss

James did not lead the army himself. He travelled as far as Lochmaben, but was too unwell to continue. The army continued for a short distance in a northeasterly direction, and reached the Solway Moss, an area of marshy, low ground by the River Esk. It was a difficult site for combat. On one side lay the River Esk, and between the Scots and safety, treacherous bogs. Lord Wharton and Lord Musgrave led the English army that moved north from Carlisle to meet the Scots. The English army was considerably smaller than the Scots army, but the Scots were disadvantaged by their lack of clear leadership. In the absence of the king, the nobles, particularly Sir James

Sinclair and Lord Maxwell, could not agree as to who should take overall command. The Scots were in disorder before the battle had properly begun, and a series of swift cavalry charges by the English under Musgrave threw the front ranks of their army into immediate panic. The defeat was swift and humiliating. Over 1200 prisoners were taken as the Scots scattered, their efforts to beat a hasty retreat hampered by the treacherous terrain. It is thought that as many were drowned in the river or lost in the marshes as were slain by the enemy troops. The victorious English returned from the battle site with all of the Scottish standards and artillery as trophies.

When he heard of his army's defeat, James was distraught. He returned to Edinburgh, then took himself to Falkland Palace, where he gave in to his illness. His wife, Mary of Guise, had had two sons by him, but both of them had died. She was now close to the end of a third pregnancy and as the king lay dying, he waited for news of the child that was to be born. When the news came, it was not what the king had prayed for. The Queen had given birth to a daughter. James V died in despair, believing that the Stewart line of Scottish monarchs was dying out.

BATTLE OF ANCRUM MOOR, 12 FEBRUARY 1545

The young Queen Mary: the rough wooing

The Scottish Catholic Church and the pro-French faction in Scotland had lost a loyal supporter when James V died. After the defeat at Solway Moss there was a growing feeling in Scotland that the pro-French policy of the Scottish government, encouraged by the Catholic Church, was benefiting the country little, and that friendlier relations with England should be fostered. When the earl of Arran was appointed governor of the kingdom instead of Cardinal Beaton, it looked as if the pro-English faction might prevail. In 1543, by the Treaty of Greenwich, it was arranged that the baby Queen Mary would be married to Edward, infant son of Henry VIII. The English king's concern for the young queen's upbringing soon made even Arran uneasy, however. Henry's wish to bring Mary up in the English court was clearly not for her own benefit. There were now fears that Scotland's independence was under threat from the ambitious English king. Arran and his supporters decided that their support for the Treaty of Greenwich had been inadvisable and changed their attitude towards Henry. Henry's response was to recommence hostilities between the two countries. In May 1544, he sent a fleet of ships up the east coast and an army northwards by land. The two forces converged at Leith where the port was laid waste. Edinburgh was then set ablaze. A force led by Arran advanced from Stirling, intent on revenge, but the English retired before a confrontation could take place. In the Scottish Borders, the English forces led by Sir Ralph Eure continued to wreak havoc. They rampaged through Kelso, Melrose, and Jedburgh with terrible savagery. Fearing for their lives, many of the Borderers went over to the English.

The battle of Ancrum Moor

In 1545, the English army, a motley crew of Englishmen, Scots Border reivers and foreign mercenaries, camped at Ancrum Moor. After several months of plundering, which had gone on without serious challenge, they were in confident mood, but the atrocities for which they were responsible could no longer be borne and a Scottish army, led by the earl of Angus, was on the way to meet them. Angus led a force of around 1200 men and as he reached Ancrum Moor, he was joined by Sir Norman Leslie, Master of Rothes, with more than 1000 troops to support him. The two forces together were outnumbered three to two by the English army, but the wily Angus was to employ a strategy that would considerably improve the odds against them.

To the west of the English army was a hill, named Gersit Law. The first appearance of the Scots to the English was made on the brow of the hill, where it looked as if they might assemble for battle. Then the cavalry were seen to dismount and turn, and the English scouts sent word to their leader that the Scots seemed to be retreating. The English army hurriedly made preparations to pursue them, hoping that by attacking the Scots as they retreated they would prevent them from gathering reinforcements and returning. They hastily reassembled and charged to the top of the hill, but the sight that greeted them was not what they had expected. The Scots cavalry had not retreated. They had merely moved round to the rear of the army, which had been assembled out of sight of the English encampment on the other side of the hill. Waiting to greet the advancing English was a wall of pikes. The English cavalry led the charge, but they were facing west and their progress was hindered by the blinding light from the setting sun in their faces. To add to their problems, the wind, blowing from the west, was blowing the smoke from both the Scots' guns and their own into their eyes. Many horses stumbled and fell in the downward rush – many more ran straight onto the pike points on the Scots front line. The Scottish guns were also being used with deadly effect. The front ranks of the English forces were driven backwards, up the slope, preventing any further advance from the troops behind them. Sir Ralph Eure attempted to rally his men again, and then again, but the Scots had sensed that victory was theirs for the taking and their assault on the beleaguered enemy was relentless. Deciding that it was safer to throw in their lot with the winning side, most of the Scots from the Borders who had been fighting with the English changed allegiance, adding to the confusion. Sir Ralph Eure was killed, along with his second-in-command, the cavalry leader, Sir George Laytoun.

Approximately 800 of the English army were slain and many more were taken prisoner. As the demoralised English forces retreated, they were set upon by local inhabitants, many of whom were women, determined to exact vengeance for their sufferings at the hands of the English raiders. One of the most famous figures from Ancrum Moor was a woman who is remembered as the Maiden of Lilliard. When she discovered that her lover had been killed by the English, she took up the sword against them herself, conducting herself in battle, it is said, with exemplary courage.

The battle drove the English raiders out of the Borders, but it did not destroy the English hopes of forcing the marriage of the young Queen Mary and Prince Edward.

Battle of Pinkie,
10 September 1547

In 1547, two years after Ancrum Moor, King Henry VIII died. His son, Edward, was only ten years old and a council, headed by Edward Seymour, earl of Hertford, was placed in charge of the country's affairs. Seymour was soon in the role of protector, as the duke of Somerset, and he made clear his intentions of forcing a union between Scotland and England by assembling an army of more than 16,000 men and a fleet of more than 60 ships – half war vessels, half supply. As the army moved northwards, nothing impeded its progress, and the fleet kept pace along the eastern coastline. They stopped at Musselburgh, less than ten miles from the capital city. In response to the threat, the earl of Arran had assembled a great army – said to have numbered anything between 20,000 and 30,000 – and now moved to meet it. The two armies drew up at either side of the River Esk, which flows north to the Firth of Forth at Musselburgh. A narrow Roman bridge afforded the only means of crossing the river easily.

Somerset's army, which numbered around 16,000, contained around 4000 cavalry, which were led by John Dudley, earl of Warwick and duke of Northumberland. These were a mixture of light cavalry, heavy cavalry (some French) and Spanish mounted arquebusiers. Offshore in the river estuary, the English ships were well armed with cannons designed for long-range firing.

The Scots army did not have a high proportion of horsemen. Most of its fighters were infantrymen – scantily-armoured Highlanders armed with two-handed swords, axes and long-bows, and Lowland levies, who generally wore better armour and were armed with pikes and swords. The infantry was rein-forced by artillery – mostly wagon-mounted arquebuses.

The Scots position was quite a strong one. They occupied a ridge of higher ground above the Esk, protected by the Firth of Forth to the left and marshland to the right. It was a position that was reasonably easy to defend, for they could not easily be outflanked. They also had a clear route for retreat, if necessary. The English encampment was made on the west of Falside Hill, approximately one and a half miles to the east of the river.

On 9 September, the eve of the battle, the Scots made a move that was to cost them dearly. A division of cavalry, under Lord Home, crossed the river and advanced to Falside Hill, goading the English into a response. More than 1000 English light cavalry rode out against them. The ensuing struggle was fierce and bloody, with losses on both sides. The Scots cavalry was driven off, severely depleted. The leader of the Scots cav-alry, Lord Home, was killed. That evening, Arran sent ambassa-dors over to the English with a proposal to stage a tournament between George Gordon of Huntly and Somerset, each sup-ported by 20 champions from their side, rather than engaging in full-scale battle. Somerset refused. He now moved some of his artillery to a different position, on the hill at Inveresk, to the right and forward from the main force, where the cannon would be within range of the left flank of the Scots. More artillery was placed on the left flank, to the west of Carberry Hill, to cover his own men as they advanced from that side.

On the following morning, the day of the battle, the Scots made a second error. Rather than waiting for the English to engage them in the strong defensive position they were hold-ing, they advanced, and crossed the river by the bridge. Somerset meanwhile was moving more artillery towards

Inveresk. Seeing this manoeuvre, the advancing Scots were drawn towards the coast, and at once began to suffer the effects of a heavy bombardment from the cannons on the English ships offshore. In order to avoid further carnage, the left flank of the Scots swung towards the centre. The speed at which the Scots were moving took the English troops aback, but the Scots were now in disorder, the left flank having come upon the centre. The English artillery on land now came into play with deadly effect, firing over the heads of their own infantry into the mass of advancing Scots. Still the Scots surged on. Then Somerset brought his cavalry into action. After repeated charges against the Scottish spears, they could not break through, but succeeded in halting the advance of the Scots. As the cavalry drew back, battered and bloodied, more cannon fire cut into the Scottish ranks, and now the English infantry came surging forward. Longbows propelled a stream of deadly arrows among the Scots and arquebusiers opened fire on the stalwart Scots pikemen. The Spanish mounted arquebusiers galloped round the Scots, firing into their midst as they went. The Scots ranks were now greatly depleted and in terrible disarray. Many were already making futile attempts to flee the combat zone when the English cavalry charged for the last time. Many of the Scots were slaughtered as they fled. More of the retreating men were drowned in the river, or lost in the marsh. When the English cavalry pursuit was finally called off, the bodies of fallen Scots lay all around.

It was one of Scotland's most tragic defeats. Arran's army had been outmanoeuvred by a more disciplined force, under the leadership of a skilful military tactician. It was a great victory for the English, but it was one that did not achieve its goal. Somerset was not able to force the Scots to hand over the young Queen Mary for marriage to Edward. She was spirited away to France, where her marriage to the child dauphin eleven years later would ensure that the Scottish–French alliance was kept intact.

Battle of Langside, 14 May 1568

Mary in Scotland

In 1554, the earl of Arran was given the title of duke of Chatelherault and persuaded to give up the regency of Scotland in favour of Mary of Guise. French influence in Scotland was growing. In 1558, the marriage between Mary Queen of Scots and Francis, the French dauphin, took place. Later that same year, Francis was declared king of Scotland. In England, the Catholic Mary Tudor, who had become queen in 1553, died and Elizabeth I had come to the throne. Catholics in France and Scotland did not recognise Elizabeth as the rightful heir, and in France, Mary was proclaimed queen of Scotland, England, and Ireland. Elizabeth I, angered by the insult, wasted little time in trying to break the Franco–Catholic influence in Scotland.

In Scotland, Mary of Guise was facing rebellion from the Scottish reformers. Protestant nobles – the 'Lords of the Congregation' banded together under the leadership of John Knox and the conflict between reformers and regent escalated. Following a sermon by John Knox at Perth in 1559, the church was stripped bare and surrounding monasteries were destroyed. In the following months, St Andrews Cathedral, Scone Abbey, the churches of Linlithgow and Stirling and many others, all fell. The Lords of the Congregation declared that Scotland was to be ruled by a committee appointed by them. In desperation, Mary of Guise summoned military reinforcements from France. The Protestant nobles turned to England for assistance and Elizabeth did not hesitate. In 1560, a fleet of English ships arrived in the Forth, followed some weeks later by an army several thousand strong and reinforced the ranks of the Scots who were laying siege to the French forces in Leith. The French held out as long as they could, but it was clear that defeat would be inevitable. Mary of Guise died in June of that year. In July, Francis, now king of France, sent ambassadors to Elizabeth, who sent them with two of her own to Scotland, and the Treaty of Leith was signed. According to the terms of the treaty, all French soldiers had to leave Scotland and no Frenchman was to be permitted to hold public office in Scotland. The last obstacle to the rise of Protestantism was removed.

Mary returned to Scotland in 1561 after the death of Francis. She was a half-French, Catholic queen, in a land where the French held no power and mass had been banned, and she was the most bitter enemy of Elizabeth of England. Fortunately, most of the Protestant nobles who had played a part in the rebellion against Mary of Guise now saw the wisdom in showing tolerance towards the queen's Catholicism, provided that Protestantism remained the established religion in Scotland. Maitland of Lethington and Mary's illegitimate half-brother James Stewart, the earl of Moray, became her closest advisors. Mary's position began to look a little more secure.

When it came to choosing a second husband, however, Mary found herself in more trouble. Her choice was Henry, Lord Darnley, son of the former exile, the earl of Lennox. Darnley was a Catholic, a fact that incurred the disapproval of the Protestant nobles. He was also a descendant of James II, which made Chatelherault, who was second in line to the throne, jealous. The earl of Moray felt equally threatened by Darnley. After the marriage, there was a revolt among the nobles, led by Moray. It was known as the 'Chaseabout Raid', because the royal force sent out to pursue the rebels never engaged them in combat.

Mary's marriage to Darnley was a disaster and her dislike of him turned to contempt when Darnley took part in the murder of David Rizzio, Mary's secretary. A brief reconciliation between Mary and Darnley resulted in the birth of a son, James, in 1566, but in January 1567, Darnley was murdered at Kirk o' Field outside Edinburgh and the earl of Bothwell, with whom Mary was becoming increasingly close, was widely believed to be responsible. Mary's actions within the next few months strengthened many people's suspicions that she, too, had played a part in the conspiracy against Darnley. In April, Bothwell made a show of taking Mary prisoner as she travelled between Stirling and Edinburgh. She barely resisted her captor and less than a month later she had married him. Her behaviour provoked outrage amongst the nobility and a full-scale rebellion led by the earl of Morton broke out. The queen's army encountered the rebel force at Carberry Hill, outside Musselburgh. No battle took place. Mary gave herself up to the rebels. Bothwell fled. Mary was taken first to Edinburgh and then to Lochleven Castle, where she was forced to abdicate in favour of her infant son, James. The earl of Moray was appointed regent.

While she was imprisoned in Lochleven Castle, Mary found she still had a degree of support. Chatelherault had no wish to see Darnley's son on the throne of Scotland. With his help, Mary engineered a daring escape from Lochleven Castle and rode to Hamilton Palace, where an army had been gathered by Chatelherault's son.

The battle of Langside

The queen's army, numbering more than 5000, made for Dumbarton Castle. If Mary succeeded in taking Dumbarton, she would command a major route to France. Regent Moray gathered an army and marched to intercept her as she passed by Glasgow. The two armies came face to face at the village of

Langside, where the regent had drawn his troops up in readiness to block the passage of Mary and her followers. The main body of Moray's army drew up on the west side of the village, while approximately 400 men were placed in positions among the houses on either side of the main road. Mary's army assembled on a small hill to the east of the village. The ensuing battle took only three-quarters of an hour and neither the cannons nor the cavalry in Mary's force played any useful part. The vanguard of Mary's army advanced in a furious charge, intent on forcing their way through the village, but were met by an immovable body of spearmen from the regent's army. Heavily armed troops from both sides, their armour, spears, and shields forming almost impregnable spiked barriers, clashed in a desperate scrum. They swayed back and forth, each side trying to break through the wall formed by the other, while missiles from either side played upon them with little effect. At last the regent's men began to gain the upper hand and the royal vanguard began to disintegrate. With no escape route available, they began to fall back on the infantry behind them, causing confusion. The remainder of the royal army could do nothing to help, for the battle arena was too confined for them to advance without harming their own men. There was no option but to concede defeat. Mary's army melted away, leaving around 300 men dead. The regent's army had lost only one man. Mary's cause was hopeless. She fled from the scene and rode to Dundrennan Abbey. From there, she sailed to England to throw herself upon the mercy of Queen Elizabeth I.

PART IV:
THE BATTLES OF
THE COVENANTING PERIOD AND
THE ENGLISH CIVIL WAR

Battle of Tippermuir,
1 September 1644

James VI: the church and the monarchy

James VI had been brought up as a Protestant, but he was also a fervent believer in the divine right of kings to absolute authority. The Presbyterian Kirk, on the other hand, believed that everyone, whether king or commoner, should be subject to God's law – i.e., the laws of the Church. This principle had been laid down in the *First Book of Discipline* in the time of John Knox: 'To discipline must all estates within this realm be subject if they offend, as well the rulers as they that are ruled.' As soon as James was old enough to rule in his own right, he began a process of gradually and cautiously reasserting royal control over the affairs of the Church. By the end of his reign, he had also begun to introduce measures to reform the ceremonial of the Church. James's policies sowed the seeds of discontent. The harvest would be reaped when his son came to the throne and attempted to continue, in more heavy-handed fashion, the process of change that his father had begun.

The early years of James's reign saw violent hostilities between opposing factions of the Scottish nobility who declared themselves either for the young king or the deposed queen. The period saw four Protestant regents – Moray, Lennox , Mar, and Morton – struggling to deal with Catholic dissenters. In 1570, Moray was murdered by a member of the Hamilton family – who were Catholics and pro-French – and Lennox was killed in a raid by the earl of Huntly on Stirling

Castle in 1571. The earl of Mar died in 1572, having tried unsuccessfully to negotiate a peace. Morton, with support from Elizabeth I, brought the worst of the troubles to an end. Edinburgh Castle, which had been held by Kirkcaldy of Grange and Maitland of Lethington since 1571, was finally taken. Lethington died suddenly after his capture and Kirkcaldy was executed.

The success of the Protestant faction did not benefit the Presbyterian Kirk. The Presbyterians' aim had been ultimately to secure all the revenues from the Catholic Church estates. The Protestant nobles, including the regent, many of whom now possessed former Church estates, had no desire to see this come to pass. In 1572, Morton oversaw the appointment of a new set of 'tulchan' bishops, who had no supervisory role within the Church, but whose duty it was to collect tithes on behalf of the lay owners of the Church estates. According to legislation passed during the reign of Queen Mary, the Kirk was entitled to one third of the revenues from Church lands. By 1573, Morton had arranged that he should make the collection of these revenues on behalf of the Kirk. The economy with which he redistributed the money further hampered the Presbyterians' plans for the growth of its ministry.

In 1578, Andrew Melville, the new leader of the Presbyterian Kirk, published the *Second Book of Discipline* and presented it to the young king. Bishops were to be abolished. The organisation of the Presbyterian Church was laid out in detail, from kirk session, to presbytery, to synod, to general assembly. More controversial was the demand that the new Kirk should take possession of all revenues from the old Church. Most controversial of all was the assertion that the Kirk government and civil government should be separate, that the king had no power to change the decrees of the Kirk, and that the Kirk had the right to decide what lay within its sphere of control. In other words, the Kirk sought control over the king and the state.

In 1581, Morton was executed for the murder of Darnley. His accuser James Stewart, captain of the royal bodyguard, was made earl of Arran. Arran and Esmé Stewart, the earl of Lennox, became the most influential figures at James's court. Their pro-French sympathies and their influence over James aroused great suspicion and resentment among the Protestant nobility. In 1582, James was seized at Ruthven by a group of Protestant nobles led by the earl of Gowrie. Lennox was banished to France and Arran was imprisoned. In 1583, James evaded his captors, and the earl of Arran was restored. An attempt by other Protestant nobles to seize Stirling Castle failed miserably. Gowrie was captured and executed and his followers fled. The Kirk had lost a potentially powerful source of support.

James now began to assert his authority over the rebellious Presbyterians. In 1584, the 'Black Acts' were passed in parliament, in a belated but emphatic response to the demands of the *Second Book of Discipline*. The Black Acts declared that the king had overall power over Church affairs, and that ecclesiastical courts could not sit without the king's consent or make binding judgments without royal ratification. The acts enforced the obedience of ministers to bishops appointed by the king and ultimately, to supreme royal authority. Criticism of the king and his family was forbidden. In 1597, following disturbances in Edinburgh over the king's right to judge the ministers, the Black Acts were re-enacted by the council, and it was declared that ecclesiastical courts could not be held in Edinburgh. James summoned a general assembly at Perth, away from the centres of dissension in Edinburgh and Glasgow, and secured its agreement to the terms of the Black Acts. At a general assembly in 1598 in Dundee it was agreed to have representatives of the Church sitting in parliament.

In 1603, James went to England to take his place on the English throne. He never returned to live in Scotland, but he did not neglect Scottish affairs and through the privy council, whose members were chosen by him, he quite successfully governed the country, as he said, with his pen. He did not take his eye off the Church. He kept firm control over the general assembly, summoning meetings only where and when he wished, and ensuring that its decisions were agreeable to him by paying generous expenses to invited ministers from the north.

Dissenting voices were silenced emphatically. Andrew Melville was imprisoned in 1606 and then exiled. Other extremists left the country or were banished. Gradually, the king saw to it that the power of his bishops was increased, consequently reinforcing his power over ecclesiastical affairs. In 1609, diocesan episcopacy became firmly re-established when an assembly in Glasgow agreed that bishops were to become moderators of the diocesan synods, with control over the ordination and deposition of ministers. The word 'presbytery' was abolished.

In 1617, the king visited Scotland and called an assembly at Perth, with the aim of introducing changes to the ceremonial of the Church to bring it more in line with the Church of England. These changes included the observance of Christian festivals, the allowance of private baptism and communion and kneeling for the sacrament.

He did not get the agreement of the assembly to all the changes, but in 1618 another assembly agreed to the reforms, known as the Five Articles of Perth. The changes were unpopular with the majority of Scottish ministers and congregations, but still there was no rebellion.

The Five Articles were ratified by parliament in 1621, but the bishops made little effort to force conformity to the changes and consequently, to a large extent, they were ignored.

Covenant and king: background to the campaigns of Montrose

In 1625, James died and his son, Charles, became king. Charles did not take long to alienate both nobility and Church in Scotland. The Five Articles remained, with few concessions. In 1625, the Act of Revocation was passed, annexing all former Church property (most of which had passed to members of the nobility after the Reformation) to the Crown. The act was amended in 1626, with the promise that compensation would be made for the annexed land. A further amendment in 1629 granted holders of Church lands permission to continue collecting revenues from the estates until they were bought by the Crown, but the damage, in terms of Charles's relations with the Scottish aristocracy, had been done. In 1635, Archbishop Spottiswoode, who had been a member of the privy council since 1605, was appointed chancellor by Charles. The appointment of a prelate to such a position of political power offended all Protestants, particularly the nobility. Strong resentment was building up against Charles, whose determination to bring the practices of the Scottish Church into line with those of England was already in evidence when he visited Scotland in 1633.

In 1636 and 1637, Charles published the *Book of Canons* and the *Book of Common Prayer*, without consulting either parliament or the general assembly, and resentment turned to rebellion. It was a foolish and dangerous move – especially as Charles was also in financial and political difficulties in England, and far from popular. When the newly appointed bishop of Edinburgh took the *Book of Common Prayer* out at a service in St Giles in July 1637, there was a riot. As far as the congregation was concerned, the use of this book meant a return to the popery that had been so strenuously rejected during the Reformation. Undeterred, Charles ordered the privy council to enforce use of the *Book of Common Prayer*.

When the privy council hesitated, he ordered that the privy council should be removed to Dundee. The discontent did not die down and, eventually, the lord advocate proposed that the dissenters should elect a committee of four nobles, four lairds, four burgesses, and four ministers to confer with the council on their behalf. This committee, known as 'the Tables', swiftly demanded that the Liturgy be withdrawn and bishops be removed from council, but the king refused and declared all protest treasonable. In reply to the king's refusal to back down, the Tables drew up a document, which became known as the National Covenant, swearing allegiance to the Protestant faith as 'the true religion', restating all anti-Catholic acts since 1560 and declaring all the measures of reform that had been introduced since the 1580s invalid.

In 1638, the National Covenant was displayed at Greyfriars in Edinburgh and copies were sent out round the country for all to sign. Thousands of signatures were gathered, although not all of them were as freely given as they might have been. Scotland, or at least the greater part of it, was behind the Covenant. At a general assembly in Glasgow later that year, the use of the *Book of Canons* and the *Book of Common Prayer* was forbidden and the bishops were abolished. The king was facing a major rebellion.

In 1639, the first 'Bishops' War' took place. A Covenanting force under the command of Alexander Leslie was led down south. Charles was unable to raise an army from England without summoning parliament, and he knew he would not get support from them on his terms. Help from his allies in Scotland, the marquises of Huntly and Hamilton, was prevented from ever setting off. The earl of Montrose met them at Aberdeen and captured Huntly. Charles had no alternative but to sign the Pacification of Berwick, agreeing to call a new general assembly and parliament. The assembly met in June 1604, and parliament met in August. Both confirmed the abolition of the episcopacy and the supremacy of the Covenant.

In 1640, the second Bishops' War took place. Charles had assembled an army – albeit a poor show of force. In response, a Scots army invaded England, and Charles, already in a weakened position against the English government, was forced to agree to ratify the decision of the Scots parliament.

Meanwhile a split was forming in the ranks of the Covenanters. The original intent of the National Covenant had not been to threaten the position of the king, to whom many of the Covenanters felt a strong loyalty, in spite of his actions. It had been drawn up to oppose his policies rather than his rule. But there was one leader among the Covenanting forces who seemed to be seeking not only the victory of the Presbyterian Church but also the downfall of the king, for his own ends. He was Archibald Campbell, earl of Argyll. James Graham, earl of Montrose, had been one of the nobles who had drawn up the National Covenant. But he had no wish to be a part in Charles's death or deposition. He was satisfied that the king had made enough concessions to the Covenanters and recognised the threat which Campbell and his followers posed to the monarchy. When the English Civil War broke out, the Scots were divided between those who supported the king and those who supported parliament. The earl of Montrose chose the former.

In the hope of securing the Presbyterian position and of uniting Scotland and England under one religion, the Scots entered into the Solemn League and Covenant with the English parliamentarians, promising their support to the parliamentarians against the king. Alexander Leslie led his troops down south and helped them secure a decisive victory at Marston Moor. The earl of Montrose, on the other hand, declared his loyalty to King Charles, was made a marquis, and was appointed king's lieutenant in Scotland. He then embarked on a year of fighting for the royal cause that was to try the Covenanters severely. His purpose was twofold. Firstly, he wanted to claim back Scotland for his king. Secondly, by causing havoc amongst the

Covenanting forces north of the border, he hoped to divert some of the Scottish troops who had gone down south to fight for the parliamentarians, and bring them back to Scotland, thereby strengthening the king's position in England.

The battle of Tippermuir

In 1644, James Graham, marquis of Montrose, marched north from his base in England. He had few men with him, but at Blair Atholl he gathered a combined force of Irish Catholics, led by Alasdair MacColla Macdonald, and Highland Scots – mostly Robertsons and Stewarts – and set forth to wage war against the Covenanters. In the year that followed, his army had a succession of victories against the Covenanting forces. These victories were remarkable not just for the swiftness and daring employed in battle, but also for the fact that he embarked upon the campaign with a force of fighting men unaccustomed to fighting together, ill-equipped, and with little supplies or money. Throughout the year, the size of his army was to wax and wane considerably, varying from 1000 to 4000. The support he got from the Highland clans was not wholehearted and frequently, having taken part in one victory, the clansmen would return to their homelands with their spoils, leaving Montrose's force depleted for the next battle. Montrose was forced to campaign constantly for others to join him as he went along, in order that he might keep the numbers of his fighting men high enough. Throughout the whole campaign, his staunchest supporters were the Irishmen and their indomitable leader, Alasdair MacColla Macdonald.

The first battle took place in September 1644 at Tippermuir in Perthshire. Montrose had no more than 3000 men under his command, and only three horses. The Irish troops under his command had only one round each for their muskets. At Tippermuir, Montrose found himself facing a force of 7000 men under the command of Lord Elcho. Elcho's men were heavily armed; Montrose's men were not. In comparison to Montrose's three horses, Elcho had a cavalry force of around 800. He also had 9 cannons.

The Covenanters were confident of a victory – perhaps too confident. Montrose's army might have been ill-disciplined and ill-equipped but they were determined. Urging his men to avail themselves of any means they could find for attacking the enemy, even if it meant picking up stones from the ground and using them as missiles and hammers, Montrose arranged them for battle.

Elcho sent forward cavalry, supported by over 100 infantry, to attack MacColla's Irishmen who were in the centre of the line. The Irishmen responded with a counter-charge of such ferocity that both cavalry and infantry were pushed back, and the panicked horses injured many of the foot soldiers as they barged among them. Montrose then urged the Highlanders into the throng, and they ran forward, roaring blood-curdling cries as they went. The speed and force of their charge caused havoc amongst the enemy, many of whom took fright and turned to flee. The cannons were useless against this kind of onslaught. The men who had been manning them abandoned their positions and ran for their lives. Montrose's army barged on with savage intensity. Picking up weapons abandoned by panicked or wounded Covenanting troops and using them against them, beating them down with stones, tearing at their opponents with their bare hands, the Highlanders showed no fear. The Covenanters had no time for a planned strategy, no room for manoeuvre. Crowded together in a chaotic jumble of horses and men, they were now moving backwards *en masse*, while Montrose's forces hacked at them mercilessly. It was nothing less than slaughter. In the ensuing carnage, Elcho lost almost one third of his army. Several hundred more were taken prisoner.

The first victory for the royalist troops was a great one. They moved on to Perth and the city surrendered. Morale was high.

But there would be little time to rest, for the Covenanters would now be out for blood. Montrose knew that in order to claim back Scotland for his king, he still had to face some formidable enemies, not least of whom was Archibald, the duke of Argyll.

BATTLE OF ABERDEEN,
13 SEPTEMBER 1644

After the battle of Tippermuir, Montrose had entertained high hopes of swelling his army with additional supporters of the royalist cause. He stayed a number of days at Perth anticipating the arrival of additional forces, but was disappointed to discover that there were few others ready to share in his optimism that the Covenanters might yet be defeated. News reached him that the duke of Argyll was on the march towards Perth against him, and he was obliged to make a move. He crossed the Tay and headed towards Dundee. Dundee refused to surrender, and rather than waste time besieging the city, Montrose carried on towards Aberdeen. A considerable number of his original army had now disappeared, having returned to their home territories with the spoils of their earlier victory, but Montrose's force was increased en route to Aberdeen by the earl of Airly and a number of his followers. Montrose now had approximately 40 horsemen and 1500 men at his disposal.

At Aberdeen, Lord Burleigh heard of Montrose's approach and assembled a force of some 3000 Covenanters, many of whom were from the clans Forbes and Fraser, ready to meet him.

Montrose forded the River Dee to the west of Aberdeen and led his men down Deeside towards the city. On 13 September, the Covenanting forces came out of the city to face Montrose, and he sent a drummer to demand surrender of the city. The

Covenanters' response was to execute the drummer. Montrose prepared to attack. As he had done at Tippermuir, he spread his men thinly in a long line, with the intention of preventing the enemy from surrounding them. He placed what little cavalry he had at either extremity of the line, along with musketeers and archers.

Battle commenced with cannon fire from the Covenanters, followed by a cavalry advance towards the royalists' right flank. Montrose ordered his horsemen from both left and right to repel the advance, and they did so with extraordinary success, in spite of their inferior numbers. He then moved his horsemen to his left flank, to oppose a second onslaught from the Covenanting forces. While the cavalry and foot of the Covenanters gathered their wits and their leaders discussed strategies for further advances, Montrose urged his entire force to make one sudden combined attack. The speed and savagery of this unexpected onslaught provoked great alarm and confusion among the Covenanting ranks and almost at once they began to retreat towards the city, pursued by their attackers. The battle had clearly been won, but Montrose's men carried on with the slaughter. Entering the city, they slew every man who came in their way. Then they set about ransacking the city, pillaging and plundering wherever they went. The conduct of the royalist supporters in the two days that followed was shameful and detracted greatly from what might otherwise have been considered an honourable victory.

BATTLE OF INVERLOCHY,
2 FEBRUARY 1645

From Aberdeen to Inverlochy

Montrose could not afford to linger in Aberdeen. The forces of Argyll were getting closer. He moved his army on to Kintore. For the next few months, Montrose kept his force on the move from place to place. The numbers of his men were alternately reduced and increased as some left, worn out by the cold and hardship, and others were induced to join up. His efforts to muster further substantial support still met with little success, and rarely did he have many more than 1000 men under his command. Campbell of Argyll followed him, slowly at first, and then more speedily, catching him by surprise at Fyvie, where a series of brief skirmishes took place. Campbell might have succeeded, had he decided to launch a full-scale attack, because Montrose's men were short of supplies and ammunition. But he remained cautious, eventually withdrawing, and Montrose and his men escaped.

The game of cat-and-mouse that the two leaders were involved in stopped for a while, when Argyll went to Edinburgh. Montrose took advantage of the Campbell chieftain's absence to move his army on towards Argyll, laying waste to Campbell territories they passed through as they went. Campbell returned to Inveraray Castle, ready to assemble his forces in response. It was now December, and the weather was bad. He did not anticipate the suddenness with which Montrose's army appeared, barely a few miles from his castle. On learning of their approach, he fled, leaving Inveraray and the surrounding lands to the mercy of the royalist forces.

The battle of Inverlochy

Montrose's army moved on from Argyll in January 1645. His intention was to proceed to Inverness and capture it, thereby inducing the clans of the north to declare for the king. As he approached Loch Ness, he received information that the earl of Seaforth was heading down to meet him, with a body of 5000 Covenanters. He might have proceeded and taken them on, but when he was at Kilcumin (Fort Augustus), he learnt that Argyll was now not many miles behind, presently stationed at Inverlochy Castle. Argyll had with him some 3000 troops. Rather than turning back towards Argyll, which would give Argyll time to prepare to meet him, Montrose opted to take him by surprise. He decided to take a circuitous and dangerous route through the hills – an extraordinary feat at that time of the year – and arrive at Inverlochy undetected.

It was a two-day march and Montrose's men had to rest up for a night to gather strength for the battle. They camped at the base of Meall-an-t'suidhe. At Inverlochy, the Covenanting forces were aware that there were some men close at hand, but they did not think that it was the whole of Montrose's army. Shots were fired between the two parties during the night, but nothing else happened.

Campbell had 2000 of his own men with him. Their ranks were further swelled by more than 1000 Lowland levies, diverted from the fighting in England, supplied by General Baillie. His next move, therefore, is puzzling. It may have been cowardice – after all, in all the time he had spent pursuing Montrose, he had never yet succeeded in engaging him in full battle. It might have been because Campbell thought that it was not Montrose at Inverlochy, but a smaller diversionary force of his men. The reason remains unclear, but Campbell left Inverlochy that night, handing over command to his cousin, Campbell of Auchinbreck, and abandoning his men to face Montrose without him for a second time.

On the morning of 2 February 1645, Montrose arranged his troops, ready for attack. As before, he stretched them wide and thin, Irishmen to right and left, Highlanders in the centre. The Covenanting forces were arranged with the Lowland levies on the flanks, the Campbell clansmen in the centre. Close by, in Inverlochy Castle itself, 50 musketeers were positioned.

The Irishmen on Montrose's left wing were the first to move, charging up to the Covenanters' right wing until they were within shooting distance before letting off a volley of musket fire, then rushing in amongst them in a solid, unstoppable mass. The force of their charge was irresistible and the Lowlanders turned and ran. Meanwhile, the Highlanders in the centre and the Irishmen on Montrose's right flank mounted their own furious assault. The ranks of the Lowlanders on the Covenanters' right wing now dispersed. The centre held firm for a while, but Montrose's troops cut into the body of them, separating them into groups, and proceeded to wreak devastation among them. Campbell men and Lowlanders alike were now in flight, pursued relentlessly by Montrose's men. When Montrose finally called a halt to the proceedings, approximately 1500 of the enemy lay dead, slain on the battlefield or in flight. Montrose's losses amounted to less than ten men. The troops in Inverlochy Castle surrendered without a fight, and the victory was complete.

BATTLE OF AULDEARN, 9 MAY 1645

After the battle of Inverlochy, Montrose moved to Elgin, where his forces were joined by a number of cavalry led by Lord Gordon. He then led his army to Dundee and took the city, but could not stay long, for news reached him that General Baillie's English troops were approaching from the south. Accordingly, he urged his men into a hasty flight northwards. To the north of him, Sir John Hurry, Baillie's second-in-command, had assembled another force. Baillie and his men held back, near Perth. Montrose moved swiftly towards Hurry's forces, but Hurry retreated, hoping to lure Montrose into an unfavourable position before making a surprise attack. Montrose's troops had reached Auldearn when Hurry gave the order to his men to turn back towards them, marching through the night and hoping to make an unexpected assault at dawn. He might have succeeded had the weather not been so damp. As they neared Auldearn, Hurry's men fired their muskets to clear them of damp powder. The noise alerted Montrose, who used the short time available to him to plan his strategy. He knew his men were vastly outnumbered by Hurry's, for Hurry had at his disposal more than 4500, of whom some 600 were on horseback. He had to rely on trickery and surprise, rather than force alone, if he were to succeed. He kept 800 infantry and 50 cavalry hidden behind a ridge to the south of the village, and 200 more cavalry hidden to the north. He placed Alasdair MacColla Macdonald with 500 of his men on the northern part of the ridge on which the village was situated, within sight of the enemy who were approaching from the west. He planted his standard in the midst of Macdonald's division, to make it appear as if these men were the main body of his troops. He also scattered a small number of infantry in the village to fire their muskets, giving the impression that it was fully occupied. Hurry's men attacked the troops on the north ridge, and succeeded in inflicting considerable damage, but they were completely taken by surprise when Montrose's men stormed in from the south, with 50 cavalry leading the charge. When the 200 cavalry who had been concealed in the north joined in the affray, the Covenanting forces were thrown into complete confusion. Montrose's tactics had paid off. The Covenanters who survived the onslaught turned to flee. As they tried to make good their escape, the royalists pursued them relentlessly for many miles, cutting down all those who faltered in their tracks.

BATTLE OF ALFORD, 2 JULY 1645

Having successfully dispatched Sir John Hurry at Auldearn, Montrose still had General Baillie to deal with. Montrose was moving towards Aberdeen, but Baillie's men were now approaching from the south and the battle could not be put off much longer. Baillie himself was cautious about taking on Montrose's army, for it was now better manned than it had ever been, and the men were confident after the run of success they had had in the past few months. But Baillie was under orders from Edinburgh, and was compelled to move in to meet them. He caught up with the royalist troops as he came to the banks of the River Don. They were across the river, looking down from a hillside above the village of Alford. Baillie advanced across the ford, thinking that Montrose's army did not look too great in numbers. Unknown to him, the bulk of the royalist force lay hidden over the brow of the hill. In total, Montrose's army nearly equalled Baillie's – some 2000 men.

Baillie's men were at once at a disadvantage on account of their lower position. Their progress was further hampered by marshy ground. First to attack were a number of cavalry, led by Lord Gordon, thundering down from Montrose's right wing towards Baillie's left, which consisted mostly of cavalry. The royalist cavalry charge was speedily followed by a horde of Irishmen on foot, who took advantage of the confusion and moved in amongst the enemy horsemen, hacking at human and horse flesh with equal ferocity. Then the cavalry on the royalist left wing charged, followed by another division of men on foot. The centre troops were the last to move in. It was devastation for Baillie's men and hundreds of them were slaughtered. Baillie was fortunate to escape with his life. Montrose's men too had suffered greater losses than in previous battles. Among the royalist casualties was the courageous Lord Gordon, whom Montrose mourned as both an ally and a friend.

BATTLE OF KILSYTH,
15 AUGUST 1645

After the battle of Alford, Montrose turned south again, and marched first to Dunkeld and then to Tullibody, where he made camp. When he continued his journey, he was careful to avoid Stirling. Within Stirling lay two threats to Montrose's army: the town was occupied by Covenanting forces and it had been struck by plague. Montrose crossed the Forth some miles above the royal burgh and made an encampment at Kilsyth, close to Colzium. His army was now quite sizable. He had approximately 4500 infantry and 500 cavalry. But Baillie's forces were on his tail. Baillie had been in Perth at a meeting of the Committee of the Scottish Estates, and he had been furnished with a force of around 6000 foot soldiers and 800 cavalry. When Montrose was setting up camp at Kilsyth, Baillie's men had reached Tullibody. They were expecting to be joined by the earl of Lanark, who had an additional 1000 infantry and 500 horse and was on the move to meet up with him.

Baillie anticipated that no encounter would take place until Lanark arrived. He continued moving closer to Montrose's army, taking up his next position only some three miles away, hoping to rest his men while they awaited Lanark's arrival.

Baillie's hopes of waiting for reinforcements were shattered. His army was accompanied by members of the Committee of the Scottish Estates, and they had the power to overrule any decisions of military strategy he might make. The committee did not want to risk the chance that Montrose might flee northwards, and determined that battle should take place before he did.

On 15 August, Baillie had his men in quite a strong position on high ground to the east of Montrose's position. Montrose's men were occupying lower ground northeast of Kilsyth, in the area now covered by Banton Loch, also known as Townhead Reservoir. The good men of the Committee of the Scottish Estates were not military tacticians, but they were anxious to assert their authority. Not satisfied with Baillie's position, they ordered him to lead his troops round the high ground to the north of Montrose's men. It was a move that was to prove fatal. Dissent broke out among the Covenanters, for the manoeuvre was clearly a dangerous one, and so the line of Baillie's men, headed by the cavalry, was already straggling and beginning to separate as they began to move towards the new position, in full view of Montrose's astounded army.

The royalists did not need to wait for a better chance. Montrose ordered his men to strip to their shirts to give them better freedom of movement and to counteract the heat of the day. His men needed no encouragement to fight when the order came to advance. A thousand Highlanders made the first charge at the head of Baillie's line, swiftly followed by a further detachment of infantry and cavalry. Then followed an attack in the centre of the line, throwing the Covenanters into complete disarray. As the whole body of Montrose's men fell about them, the Covenanters gave way to general panic and frantic attempts at retreat. More than half of their infantry fell at the hands of the fearsome Highlanders. Baillie was driven into retreat with many of his cavalry following. He managed to escape, but several of his horsemen became trapped in the Dullater bog and were lost. The victory was achieved with very few losses for the royalist forces, but the death toll on the Covenanters' side was enormous. When news of the battle reached the earl of Lanark, he knew that further resistance to Montrose's fury was useless. He turned back and his men dispersed.

BATTLE OF PHILIPHAUGH,
13 SEPTEMBER 1645

From Kilsyth to Philiphaugh

Kilsyth was a decisive battle for Montrose, leaving him in a position of supremacy in Scotland. But things were not going well for King Charles I in England, and the royalist army had suffered a terrible defeat at the battle of Naseby. There was little chance that his majesty would be returning north to follow up on Montrose's successes. Montrose was determined to move south to support his king, but events were beginning to turn against him.

The Highlanders who had made up the better part of the royalist army began to disperse, returning to their own lands to share their booty with their families and to defend their territory and kinfolk against possible reprisals from the Campbell clan or their supporters. Montrose's force was dwindling daily, in spite of his valiant attempts to enlist more recruits as he travelled southwards through the Borders. And when news of his victory at Kilsyth reached the Scottish army serving on the side of the parliamentarians in England, it was decided that Montrose's move south had to be stopped at all costs, and with all speed. General David Leslie was sent to deal with the problem, heading a force of 4000 men. He moved swiftly north over the border, and on receiving information that Montrose was at Philiphaugh, moved in for the attack before Montrose had time to prepare any sort of response.

The battle of Philiphaugh

Despite having an army considerably reduced in strength and numbers, Montrose remained determined to maintain his progress southwards to link up with the beleaguered Charles. He was confident that for the moment at least Scotland was his, and that he was in no imminent danger. He set up camp at Philiphaugh near Selkirk in a reasonably good position strategically, defended by the River Ettrick on one side and the hills on the other. His scouts gave no report of any threat to the army's safety in the area, and so Montrose left his men at the encampment and went to Selkirk with a small escort to spend the night.

Montrose had been wrong to feel so optimistic. Leslie was advancing with great speed, and had picked up additional reinforcements on his way. He now had around 6000 troops at his command, and his intention was to take Montrose's army by surprise. He divided his force in two, each coming upon the royalist encampment from a different side, and they moved in for an early morning attack, their approach being made all the easier by a thick mist that enshrouded the area and concealed them. When they made their attack, the royalists were completely unprepared, and the force of Leslie's army coming down upon them was almost irresistible. The royalists put up a desperate fight without their leader, but were being killed in their hundreds. Montrose arrived on the scene to find the remains of his men being forced backwards. His last-ditch attempt to mount a cavalry charge against Leslie's men was valiant, but doomed to failure. Urged on by some of his most senior men to escape, he rode away from the scene. The men he left behind him surrendered.

The survivors of the battle might have been better off if they had stayed and fought, or fled the scene. Leslie herded them up and marched them to Newark Castle, two miles away, and there gave orders for every last man to be shot. Not content with this atrocity, the Covenanters also captured around 80 women and children, camp followers, who had managed to get as far as West Lothian. These poor unfortunates were drowned in the River Avon.

The battle of Philiphaugh put a tragic end to Montrose's 'year of miracles'. Within two months of having taken Scotland for the king, he had lost it again, and had been forced to leave the country for Norway.

Battle of Preston, 17 July 1648

Charles attempts a comeback

The Scots had lent their support to the parliamentarians in the English Civil War in return for a pledge that the Presbyterian Church would become dominant in England. Now, with the rise in power of Cromwell and the Independents, it was unlikely that the pledge would be fulfilled. In 1646, Charles I had given himself up to the Scottish army in England, but although he agreed to establish Presbyterianism in England for five years, he still refused to sign the Covenant. In 1647, the Scots handed Charles over to the English parliament and their army left England having received an agreed sum of money as part of their arrears of pay.

King Charles was taken captive by the English army, but escaped to the Isle of Wight. By this time he had made contact with Scotland again, and in a secret treaty known as the Engagement, made with the earls of Lauderdale and Lanark, he agreed to establish Presbyterianism in England for three years and confirm the Covenant in parliament, in exchange for military support. The Scottish Presbyterians were now divided. Some believed that through the king, Presbyterianism might still be established in England and opted to support him. Others, chiefly the leaders of the Presbyterian Church, were against the engagement and made strenuous efforts to persuade military leaders not to take up arms for the king. In consequence, in July 1648, the duke of Hamilton led an army that was considerably smaller than he had hoped for across the border to join the forces of the English royalists.

The battle of Preston

Cromwell himself led an army of more than 9000 to meet the royalists at Preston. The royalist forces were not assembled all together. The duke of Hamilton and the English royalists were in Preston, but a large body of infantry under Baillie had already crossed the Ribble to the south of the town. Middleton's cavalry were close to Wigan, 15 miles south of Preston. Another body of troops, Irishmen under the command of Monro, were still 30 miles north of Hamilton's force. On 17 July, Cromwell's men attacked the duke of Hamilton's army, and after a fierce battle, managed to take Preston. Hamilton crossed the Ribble with his force severely depleted and joined up with Baillie. They then marched south, hoping to meet with Middleton and the cavalry. They came together at Wigan and the decision was taken to move on to Warrington.

Cromwell's army was hard on their heels, and the Scots lost more cavalry and infantry as they fled from Wigan. The third battle front was at Winwick, close to Warrington. On 19 July, Baillie's infantry were drawn up to face the English as they advanced, and the courageous stand taken by the Scots pikemen and musketeers held back Cromwell's army for several hours. Repeated charges by Cromwell's men eventually wore the Scots down and they were driven back to the Mersey, where Baillie surrendered. The duke of Hamilton was now left in command of a very small force of infantry and cavalry. There was no hope of victory now. On the 25 July, he surrendered to Cromwell at Uttoxeter. He was condemned to death by the English parliament and beheaded.

The battle was a triumph for the extreme Presbyterians in Scotland. The Whiggamores, or Whigs, Presbyterians from the southwest who had strenuously opposed the Engagement, marched to Edinburgh and, with the support of cavalry from Cromwell's army, drove out the Committee of Estates and assumed power. In 1649, the Act of Classes was passed. Offenders were divided into three classes, according to the degree of support they had given to Montrose and the royalist cause, and the Engagement. The most serious offenders were barred from holding office for life. The second class were barred for ten years and the third, for five years.

Battle of Dunbar,
2–3 September 1650

In January 1649, Charles I was executed. His exiled son Charles was proclaimed king in Scotland. Charles II would have no authority until he signed the Covenant and Solemn League and Covenant. On the orders of the new king, Montrose made an attempt to muster enough men for a royalist uprising in the Highlands, but it was a dismal failure and resulted in Montrose's execution. Charles hesitated no longer. In June 1650, he signed the Covenant and Solemn League and Covenant and came to Scotland.

Meanwhile, in England, Cromwell had come to power as protector and was looking to consolidate his position. He had subdued the Irish in a vicious campaign in 1649 and now was turning his attentions to Scotland. In July 1650, he led an army northwards. In spite of the threat from Cromwell, the extreme Presbyterians continued what the Act of the Classes had begun. Anyone who had served under Montrose or the duke of Hamilton was forbidden to serve in the army. The resulting purge severely diminished the size of the force that could be called upon to serve the new king and took away many of its most able leaders. Nonetheless, the army that was mustered under the command of David Leslie to prevent Cromwell from advancing on Edinburgh was twice the size of Cromwell's force.

Throughout August, Leslie's army kept Cromwell at bay.

Gradually the long campaign took its toll on Cromwell's army, and weakened by sickness and fatigue, they moved back down the east coast towards Berwick. Leslie intercepted them at Dunbar and taking command of Doon Hill, blocked off the path of their retreat to England. Leslie was in a strong position. His force outnumbered Cromwell's two to one, and was placed on superior ground. If Cromwell attacked, he was unlikely to win. Cromwell had ships off the coast, but Leslie's army was well positioned to cut off any attempt to reach them. Cromwell's army was already weak and supplies were dangerously low; given time, it might have been persuaded to surrender. But whatever military strategy Leslie might have adopted, the members of the Committee of the Estates who accompanied the Scots army were not for waiting, and it was they who had the final say. On the night of 2 September, by order of the Committee of the Estates, Leslie began to lead his army down from their secure position on Doon Hill.

At first light on 3 September, Cromwell seized his opportunity. The Scots army had not had time to draw up in battle formation when the cavalry of the Cromwellian army charged against them. The Scots cavalry, ill-prepared for the onslaught, put up what resistance they could but in less than an hour most of them had fallen, along with a large number of supporting infantry. The rest of the Scots army put up very little resistance. Most of them scattered and fled, pursued relentlessly for several miles by Cromwell's men. Cromwell himself estimated that 3000 Scots were killed in the battle. A further 10,000 were taken prisoner.

Battle of Worcester,
3 September 1651

After the defeat at Dunbar, Cromwell was able to take control of Edinburgh. The extreme Presbyterians turned on the Committee of the Estates, disowned Charles, and formed an army of their own. After a humiliating defeat at Hamilton, by a force led by Cromwell's lieutenant Lambert, they lost support and credibility. The way was clear for the more moderate Presbyterians to take control. On New Year's Day, Charles II was crowned at Scone. Shortly after that, the Act of Classes was repealed, and the way was clear for the king to build up a stronger army. There was little left for Charles to rule. England was lost to him and Cromwell was in possession of all of southern Scotland.

Cromwell now made a move to extend his control to the north of Scotland. Stirling was holding out strongly against him, blocking one route to the north. Cromwell decided that he would have to advance through Perth. At the beginning of August 1651, his army captured Perth and he was anticipating an encounter with Leslie's army.

It seems that Leslie had also hoped to fight Cromwell in Scotland, on familiar territory, but Charles II was more anxious to make his mark in England, to rekindle the royalist cause there, and gather more support. Shortly after he had taken Perth, Cromwell learned that the Scots army was moving into England. General Monck was left in charge of an army in Scotland, to continue where Cromwell had left off. Cromwell hurried after the Scots, gathering reinforcements for his own army as he went. He caught up with the Scots at Worcester, where Charles had stopped to rest his men and gather provisions.

The Scottish army numbered around 16,000. Cromwell had twice as many men under his command. He sent one division, under Fleetwood, across the Severn to attack the city from the south while he launched an artillery attack from the east. Bridges of boats were constructed across the Severn and the River Teme to the south of the town to enable troops to advance. Charles's army came out of the city to meet the advance but was driven back in. In a hard-fought battle, much of it hand-to-hand fighting, lasting several hours, Cromwell's army managed to wrest Worcester from the hands of the Scots, sending them into retreat through the north of the town. King Charles escaped and eventually made his way to France, but thousands of prisoners were taken, including most of the Scots military leaders.

The journey to Worcester had been a futile exercise for the Scots and for Charles. The royal cause had got no further south of the border, and while the king and the army had been engaged at Worcester, Cromwell's able lieutenant, General Monck, had sacked Dundee and taken the members of the Committee of Estates prisoner. Cromwell now had total control of Scotland.

BATTLE OF RULLION GREEN, 26 NOVEMBER 1666

The Restoration, and the renewal of the Covenanters' struggles

Cromwell's rule brought eight years of peace and relative stability to Scotland. In 1658, Cromwell died, and Charles II was restored to the throne in 1660. Charles displayed no desire to return to Scotland himself and appointed the earl of Lauderdale as secretary of state and John Middleton as royal commissioner. The king, who had signed the Covenant ten years before, and who promised on his restoration to protect the Church as established by law, now began to demonstrate his true feelings towards the Presbyterian Church. The Restoration Parliament of 1661 passed a Rescissory Act, nullifying all legislation since 1633. The 'Church as established by law' was now the Episcopalian Church. Within a year, episcopacy had been re-established and the Covenant had been declared illegal. An Act of Indemnity passed in 1662 offered pardons to hundreds of prominent Presbyterians upon payment of fines, but others were not so fortunate. The marquis of Argyll and Johnston of Warriston were put to death.

The practice of appointing ministers in the Scottish Church through congregational vote, which had been in effect since 1649, was abolished and lay patronage was reintroduced. All ministers were required, within six months, to have their appointments reconsidered by the lay patron of the local kirk and the bishop of the diocese. In February 1663, on the day by which all were supposed to have conformed to the new conditions, almost 300 ministers resigned. Their places were taken by Episcopalian ministers, but the newcomers, inexperienced and unpopular, found themselves with poor congregations. Most of the ousted clergy took their ministry into the open air, and their congregations followed. Religious meetings, or 'conventicles', were held in the countryside. The government's response to this defiance was to impose fines on those who attended these meetings, or who simply refused to attend church, and to enforce payment of the fines using the military. In the southwest of Scotland, home of the Whigs, the most extreme of the protesters, the persecution resulted in uprising. Sir James Turner, leader of the dragoons who were employed in tracking down the Covenanters, was taken prisoner in Dumfries. His captors gathered a large band of supporters and, in November 1660, almost 3000 of them set out to march on Edinburgh.

The battle of Rullion Green

The rebel force was unable to gather any more support as it moved towards Edinburgh. The long march in desperately cold and muddy conditions took its toll and soon the 3000 had dwindled to 1000. They reached Colinton, only a few miles from the capital city, but their determination had been undermined by the lack of support they had received and they were tired and weak. The decision was taken to turn and cross back over the Pentland Hills. They did not get far. Sir Thomas Dalziel was in pursuit of them with a strong body of men, and caught up with them at Rullion Green near Penicuik. Dalziel's force outnumbered the Conventiclers and his men were fitter and better armed. In a short but bloody battle, the Conventiclers were overwhelmed. Approximately

50 were killed in battle. More than 30 of those who were captured were executed and many more were transported to the
West Indies. Two men were tortured with the 'boot' before
being put to death.

BATTLE OF DRUMCLOG, MAY 1679

1666–1679: Repression and resistance

Rullion Green did not put an end to the Conventicler's protests. The earl of Lauderdale's approach to the rebellion had two sides. On the one hand, he was willing to show moderation to those who could be persuaded to accept some compromise. In 1669, he persuaded Charles II to issue a Letter of Indulgence, which allowed ministers who had lived peaceably to return to their parishes. In 1672, a second Letter of Indulgence brought 90 more ministers back into the church, appointed to 58 selected parishes. These measures split the ranks of the Conventiclers. Those who were drawn back into the Church through the Indulgences were condemned by the more extreme protestors, who became even more defiant in their attitude. Lauderdale was unwilling to show any leniency when dealing with these persistent rebels. In 1670, a bill was passed making attendance at a conventicle treasonable. Those who preached at the meetings were liable to be sentenced to death.

Repression of the Conventiclers continued over the next few years. Landowners were held responsible for the behaviour of their tenants and penalised heavily if conventicles were held on their land, a measure that added to the unrest. In 1678, a mixed force of 9000 Highlanders and Lowlanders was moved to the southwest of Scotland, seat of the rebellion, to help with dispersing the conventicles and punishing the offenders. The Conventiclers became more determined in their defiance and more organised in their response to the persecution. On 3 May 1679, a group of Covenanters dragged Archbishop Sharp of St Andrews from his coach and murdered him. In Rutherglen, on 29 May, in an act of open defiance, another group publicly burnt copies of the acts of government that had overthrown the Covenant. It was inevitable that the conflict would escalate.

The battle of Drumclog

One of the most prominent figures in the government army was John Graham of Claverhouse, a very capable military leader whose zeal in carrying out his duties in stamping out the Covenanting revolt was to become notorious. When news reached him that a large conventicle was holding meetings at Drumclog, he set off with a body of troops to disperse them. The government troops were well armed and well disciplined, but the Covenanters, whose numbers were greater, had the advantage of familiarity with the marshy terrain. They too were well armed and they were well-prepared for the attack. Claverhouse's horsemen soon found themselves in difficulty on the soft and sodden ground, and the Covenanters laid into them ferociously, killing a great many of them and sending Claverhouse and the rest of the survivors into flight.

The victory spurred the Covenanters on to greater things. Several thousand stormed Glasgow, drove out the occupying garrison and by 6 June had taken command of the city. Their success was to be short-lived. Within two weeks the tide would turn against them.

BATTLE OF BOTHWELL BRIDGE,
22 JUNE 1679

The duke of Monmouth, the illegitimate son of Charles II, was given command of a force several thousand strong and was marching from England to deal with the insurgence. The royal army was further reinforced as it advanced towards Glasgow by troops from Scotland. Monmouth had the support of several able military leaders, including Claverhouse, the earl of Linlithgow, the earl of Airlie, Lord Mar, and the earl of Home. Although the Covenanters had the advantage of position, they were not so numerous. In addition to this, disputes had broken out between the moderates and extremists, and the differences between the two sides threatened their unity as a fighting force. The moderates were prepared to attempt to negotiate with Monmouth, and two envoys were sent out to discuss terms with him. But when they returned with Monmouth's request for the Covenanters to lay down their arms, the extremists would have nothing to do with it. A violent confrontation was inevitable.

The two sides faced each other across the River Clyde – the royal army, well disciplined, well armed and well organised, the Covenanters disorganised and demoralised by internal disagreement. Spanning the river between the two armies was Bothwell Bridge, which was held by a force of around 300 Covenanters, most of whom were moderates. For more than two hours this gallant band of men held the bridge against the royal army, but they became exhausted with the effort and were running out of ammunition. Their pleas for reinforcements were not answered. No help came to them from the main body of Covenanters. When the order was given for them to fall back they had no choice but to obey. As soon as they fell back from the bridge, Monmouth began sending his army across. The royal artillery was moved across and from their new position on the Covenanters' side of the river the cannons thundered out a deadly volley.

Panic broke out among the Covenanters and they began to scatter. The horsemen of the royal army moved in amongst them, hacking at them indiscriminately and pursuing them as they fled. Several hundred were killed and more than 1000 were taken prisoner. The prisoners were force-marched to Edinburgh. Two ministers were hanged in the city. Five of the prisoners were taken to Magus Moor, where Archbishop Sharp had been murdered, and hanged. The majority of the captives were herded into an enclosure in the churchyard of Greyfriars, where they were kept under guard for several months. Exposed to the elements and denied all but the most meagre of provisions, many of them died. By November, a few hundred had been freed in exchange for a promise that they would never again take up arms against the king. Some had been fortunate enough to escape. Nearly 300 were sentenced to transportation to the West Indies. They were marched to Leith and crammed into the hold of a ship. In the cramped and airless conditions below decks, it is unlikely that many of them would have survived the voyage, but the ship did not get far. It was wrecked off the coast of Orkney and most of the prisoners drowned.

It was only a relatively small number of Covenanters who kept up the armed struggle after the battle of Bothwell Bridge. These extremists, named Cameronians after their leader Richard Cameron, continued to hold secret meetings in the hills. Richard Cameron was killed in 1680, but his followers remained fixed in their purpose. In 1681, they solemnly excommunicated the king, the duke of York, the duke of Monmouth, and other government leaders. In 1684, they issued the 'Apologetical Declaration', in which they claimed justification for killing those who persecuted them, and as a result, faced further repression. This was the period known as the 'killing time', when many extremists were executed by members of the military commissioned to hunt them down. Gradually the resistance of the Covenanters was worn down.

PART V:
THE JACOBITE RISINGS

BATTLE OF KILLIECRANKIE, 27 JULY 1689

James VII

When Charles II died in 1685, he was succeeded by his brother James, a Roman Catholic. The way had been prepared for James's succession in 1681, when parliament declared that the sovereign need not be a Protestant. As lord high commissioner, James had played a part in the repression of the Covenanters. After he came to the throne, it became clear that his sympathies were more pro-Catholic than anti-Presbyterian. In 1687, James issued his first Letter of Indulgence, suspending all the laws against Catholics. He balanced this by another Letter of Indulgence in 1688, giving Presbyterians similar freedoms, but his opponents were nonetheless suspicious. They believed that the new king's ultimate intention was to reimpose Roman Catholicism on the country. As it turned out, however, it was events in England that forced James from the throne. Opponents to his attempts to enforce religious tolerance there called upon William of Orange, husband of James's daughter, Mary, to invade England. James offered no opposition and fled into exile.

In March 1689, the Convention of the Estates met in Edinburgh and issued a Claim of Right, declaring that it had the power to depose the sovereign. James was deposed and the Crown was offered to William and Mary, on condition that episcopacy was abolished. William agreed, provided that there would be no religious persecution. Refusing to renounce their loyalty to James, around 200 Episcopalian ministers resigned from their posts.

There was little open sympathy for the ousted king in the Lowlands of Scotland. But there was still a large proportion of Scots, including Catholic Highland chiefs in the north and the dispossessed Episcopalians, who were anxious to see James restored to the throne. Graham of Claverhouse, now Viscount Dundee, did not hesitate. Travelling to the north, he began negotiating with the clan chiefs to rally support for James's cause.

The battle of Killiecrankie

Dundee's task was considerably hampered by feuding and suspicion between the clans, but by July he had managed to muster an army of around 2000 men – his own small force of cavalry, supported by Camerons, Macdonells of Glengarry, Macdonalds of Clanranald, Macleans, and a number of Irish recruits. The government force that was sent out to meet him under the command of Hugh Mackay numbered around 4000 – 3000 infantry and four troops of horse. The Jacobites, as James's supporters were now known, had already taken Blair Castle and Mackay intended to recover it. As Mackay's force marched from Perth towards Blair, Dundee's army moved southeast from Blair towards the Pass of Killiecrankie to intercept him. When Mackay had reached the northern end of the pass, he halted his army on level ground. The River Garry was to his left. To the right, the ground sloped upwards. On the higher ground to the right of Mackay's army, Dundee had drawn up his Highland army. Mackay realised he was in a very vulnerable position, but a battle could not be avoided. He turned his men to face their enemy and moved them to a slightly better defensive position higher up. Rather than assembling his troops in a block, he spread them out thinly, drawing out the line of battle in an attempt to prevent Dundee's men from moving round their flank and attacking from behind. Dundee re-formed his own lines to compensate. The two armies waited, facing each other in this way, for some time.

Shortly after seven o'clock in the evening, Dundee gave his men the order to advance. The battle was to be brutally short. After an initial exchange of gunfire, the Highlanders drew their swords and charged headlong down the slope. The charge was so swift that Mackay's troops had little time to reload their muskets after firing. With many of their guns empty and little else to defend themselves they faced the full fury of the Highland swordsmen bearing down upon them. Their ranks rapidly began to disintegrate as many of them started to run. Mackay tried to rouse the cavalry into a counter-attack to no avail. As his panic-stricken troops tried to flee, many of them fell in the confusion. Mackay himself managed to survive the battle, but he retreated to Aberfeldy at the head of only a few hundred men.

The Jacobites had won their first victory, but it was not one that they would be able to exploit. The fearless Viscount Dundee had been killed by musket fire in the midst of the affray and his army was left without a strong leader. Colonel Cannon, who took over from Dundee, did not possess the same strength of character or military prowess. Nor was he ready to lead an army of mutually suspicious clansmen. After the battle of Killiecrankie, the Jacobite numbers swelled to around 5000. In August, Cannon led them to Dunkeld, which was occupied by Lieutenant-Colonel William Cleland and a force of around 1200 government soldiers – the newly formed Cameronians. In spite of their superiority in numbers, and in spite of repeated assaults on the town, the Jacobites were unable to force the Cameronians to surrender and had to admit defeat. Dispirited by their failure, many of the Highlanders returned to their homes. One year later, after another defeat at Cromdale, the remnants of the Jacobite army in Scotland dispersed.

Things might have ended differently if the deposed King James had lent his support to the struggle in Scotland, but his efforts were directed elsewhere. In 1689, he had gone to Ireland, with financial and military support from France. In July 1690, his army was heavily defeated at the battle of the Boyne and he retreated once more to France. He did not return to reclaim his throne. In 1701, James VII and II died and the Jacobites proclaimed his 13-year-old son, James Francis Edward Stewart, as the new, rightful king.

THE MASSACRE OF GLENCOE,
13 FEBRUARY 1692

In spite of the failure of the Jacobite forces to follow up on their success at the battle of Killiecrankie, William III was aware that his position as king might still face a threat from the Highlands, where there were still several chiefs who supported the Jacobite cause. William chose not to deal with the problem in person – he had not set foot in Scotland and seemed to have no intention of doing so. In 1691, he agreed to give the earl of Breadalbane money with which to buy the allegiance of the most powerful chiefs. An amnesty would be granted to all those who submitted to William III as king, and a deadline, 1 January, 1692, was set for the chiefs to take an oath of allegiance. Signatures from all the chiefs, except one, Alexander Macdonald of Glencoe, were received on time. Macdonald held out until the last moment and when he finally travelled to Inveraray to take the oath, bad weather prevented him from reaching the town until 6 January.

Breadalbane was a leader of Clan Campbell, and the Macdonalds of Glencoe had been a thorn in his side for a long time. He was keen to take the opportunity to avenge himself for past wrongs. Although both he and Sir James Dalrymple of Stair, secretary of state, were well aware that Macdonald had signed the oath of allegiance, the information was not passed on to the privy council. The king's signature was obtained on a warrant ordering the extirpation of the Macdonalds and at the beginning of February, Campbell of Glenlyon was sent to Glencoe with a company of men. The laws of Highland hospitality were stronger than any suspicions that the Macdonalds might have had towards their Campbell visitors and they took them into their houses. On the night of 13 February, the Campbells attacked the Macdonalds in their homes. Thirty-eight of the Macdonald clan, including the chief and his son, were killed and the rest fled for their lives in the snow.

The massacre provoked feelings of outrage throughout the Highlands. In the years that had gone before, there had been countless lives lost in the constant warring between the clans, but the events at Glencoe had broken the ancient laws of hospitality in the king's name. Although they kept their peace in the meantime, many of the chiefs turned against William III. When news of the massacre reached the Lowlands, Jacobite sympathisers went to great lengths to publicise the affair, bringing down public censure on William for his laxity in not bringing the perpetrators of the outrage to justice. William damaged his reputation further by the slowness of his response. A proper investigation of the affair was not carried out until 1695. Parliament declared that the killings had been wrong, but cleared the king of any blame. Dalrymple was removed from office, and Breadalbane was imprisoned, but never brought to trial. The Jacobites and their sympathisers were not alone in feeling that justice had not been done.

Battle of Sheriffmuir, 13 November 1715

The risings of 1708 and 1715

The peace that reigned in the years between 1692 and 1715 was an uneasy one. The countries of Scotland and England had been united under one monarch since 1603, but had not shared their government. Scotland kept its own parliament and its own laws. Sharing a monarch with England had not brought Scotland any advantages in trade or prosperity. Resistance to a parliamentary union, however beneficial that might prove to the country's wealth, was still strong. In 1702, William of Orange died. His wife, Mary, had been childless when she died in 1695. William was succeeded by Mary's sister, Queen Anne. In 1707, five years after Anne came to the throne, the Treaty of Union was signed after protracted negotiations, and became law in May of that year. Although there was opposition to the union, chiefly among the Jacobites and the Country Party, led by the duke of Hamilton, it was neither strong enough nor adequately organised to prevent it. Scotland and England now shared a parliament and currency but the two countries maintained separate churches and legal systems. Feelings of resentment were still running high.

James Edward Stewart had the support of Louis XIV of France, who recognised him as the rightful king of Scotland, England, and Ireland. In 1708, the French king provided James with 6000 men and a fleet of ships with which to invade Scotland. Ill-feeling was running high in Scotland following

the union of the parliaments, and James and Louis were confident that they would find no lack of support for the Jacobite
cause when James landed in Scotland. The enterprise was a
failure. First of all the French fleet, under the command of
Admiral Forbin, was blockaded in Dunkirk by a squadron of
the British navy. When it did manage to evade the British ships
and cross to the Firth of Forth in treacherous weather conditions, it was met by another group of British ships. James was
anxious to land and take his chances in Scotland, but the
French commander thought better of it and withdrew his
fleet. There were no further attempts to restore the Stewarts to
the throne until 1715. When the Treaty of Utrecht brought an
end to the War of the Spanish Succession in 1713, Louis XIV
was compelled, according to the terms of the treaty, to expel
James from France.

In 1714, Queen Anne died and George of Hanover succeeded to the British throne. Once again, Jacobites in Great
Britain and on the Continent set plans in motion for an uprising that was to take place simultaneously in England and in
Scotland. The rising was blighted by misfortune, lack of coor-
dination and poor leadership.

The leader of the rising in Scotland was the earl of Mar. A
former Whig, who had helped the earl of Queensberry push
through the Act of Union, Mar earned the nickname 'Bobbing
John' for his ability to change sides when it suited him. He
was not a particularly able military leader and his indecision
would play no part in the failure of the rising. In August 1715,
Mar summoned the Highland chiefs to talks at a hunting party
on his estates. On 6 September, the Scottish standard was
raised at Braemar and James Francis Edward Stewart was proclaimed king. The rising had already suffered one setback at
this stage, for a few days earlier Louis XIV had died, and the
Jacobites could no longer hope for support from France.

By the end of September, Mar had taken Perth and was virtually in command of all of Scotland north of the River Tay.

He had an army of around 12,000 men at his disposal. The commander of the government troops, the duke of Argyll, led a force of less than 2000. If Mar had seized the opportunity to act when the odds were in his favour, things might have turned out differently. But Mar was unwilling to move south without a guarantee of support from that direction. He delayed, hoping for news of the arrival of James and an invasion in England. He was eventually forced to take action in October when he heard of the risings in southwest Scotland and the north of England. Keeping the main body of his army in Perth, he sent almost 2000 men south under the command of Mackintosh of Borlum, to join up with Kenmure, leader of the rebellion in the southwest, and the English Jacobites. Another company of soldiers was sent to Argyll, to attack the duke of Argyll's stronghold at Inveraray and try to divert Argyll from his position at Stirling.

The action in Argyll was unsuccessful. Inveraray could not be taken and the duke of Argyll, secure in the knowledge that his territory was safe, remained in central Scotland. The contingent that moved south fared little better. Mackintosh led his men down the east coast. He should have continued directly south, to join up with Kenmure and the English Jacobites and lead them north. This would have placed Argyll as the meat in the sandwich, between Mar's men to the north and Mackintosh's to the south. But Mackintosh diverted from his course at Edinburgh. Spies had alerted Argyll to the fact that Mackintosh was advancing on the capital, and Mackintosh then found himself engaged in a day of time-wasting and fruitless skirmishing around the port of Leith before continuing his journey to the border.

Mar waited on at Perth, gathering further reinforcements for his army, while Mackintosh led his men to Kelso, to meet up with Kenmure and the English Jacobites. His proposal that the three forces should join together and march north was rejected. Forster, leader of the English Jacobites, wanted an invasion of

England and would not be put off. Mackintosh agreed to support him, although several hundred Highlanders in his army refused to cross the border and deserted. The combined Scottish and English Jacobite army marched towards Preston, hoping to link up with more Jacobite troops in Lancashire. Their progress was unopposed, but when they reached Preston they found that they were caught between one government force led by Carpenter and another led by General Wills. They barricaded themselves in Preston and, on 12 November, Wills's army attacked, but was unable to force a way past the Jacobite barricades and suffered heavy losses. The next day, Carpenter's force arrived and the combined government army surrounded the town and sealed off all escape routes. On 14 November, the Jacobites were forced to surrender.

The battle of Sheriffmuir

On the same day as defeat at Preston became inevitable, events in Scotland were also taking a turn for the worse. The indecisive Mar had waited too long. On 9 November, he had been compelled to call a council of war and the decision was taken to cross the Forth and move south. After having been considerably reduced in size with the departure of Mackintosh's army, his army was now almost back to its former strength, but Argyll had also had time to muster additional troops and now commanded an army of 4000 soldiers. Mar left Perth on 10 November. Argyll, informed by spies of Mar's movements, marched to meet him. He drew up his army on Sheriffmuir, a mile northeast of Dunblane, and blocked the route along which Mar was proceeding from Perth to Stirling. The two armies met on 13 November.

The duke of Argyll commanded the right wing of the royal army and General Whetham took the left wing. The Jacobite army, partially concealed by undulations in the land, extended far past Whetham's left wing, but Argyll was unaware of the danger. He led his side of the army in a charge on the Jacobite left wing and although their advance was hindered initially by Jacobite gunfire, they succeeded in driving the Highlanders back. Meanwhile, however, the Jacobite right wing had charged the government left, and had sent them reeling back towards Stirling. Argyll called his own right wing back to confront Mar's left wing. Both armies had now been reduced to around two-thirds of their original size – Argyll had around 1000 men still in the field, while Mar had 4000. It was late in the afternoon and the light was beginning to fade and although Mar had the advantage of greater numbers on his side, he refused to attack. Argyll withdrew to Dunblane. Mar headed back to Perth.

The battle itself had been inconclusive – both sides claimed that they were the victors of the day – but Mar's failure to secure a decisive victory left his Highland troops demoralised. His army began to dwindle in numbers. Argyll, on the other hand, had only a few weeks to wait until reinforcements under General Cadogan came from Holland, swelling his army by some 6000 men. There was little chance of the Jacobites successfully moving south again, even under strong leadership. As it was, with Mar as their leader, there was no chance.

Months before, when the plans for the rebellion had been in their earliest stages, it was intended that 'the Pretender' would land in the southwest of England and lead the rising there. But the government had been forewarned, and before James could set sail for England, the rising in the southwest had been stopped in its tracks. Forced to pin his hopes on the northern rising, James had travelled from St Malo to Dunkirk, to sail for Scotland. On 23 December, when his cause was already lost, he landed at Peterhead. He travelled to Perth early in January 1716 to find Mar and a dispirited army of less than 5000 men. The news of Preston and Sheriffmuir depressed him further. The Pretender was neither an inspiring nor an inspired leader of men and disheartened as he was by the lack of success of his supporters so far, he lacked the spirit to rouse the rebels to further efforts on his behalf. A coronation had been planned at Scone on 23 January, but it was put off. Argyll and Cadogan were advancing from the south, and the Jacobites decided to retreat. With Argyll hard on their heels, they crossed the Tay to Dundee and moved on to Montrose. There, James slipped away from his army and boarded a ship for France. The remnants of the Jacobite army, with Argyll still in pursuit, moved on to Ruthven, where they dispersed in February.

Battle of Glen Shiel, 10 June 1719

The rising of 1719

It was the Spanish government that kindled the first flames of the Jacobite rising of 1719, in retaliation for British attacks on the Spanish fleet off the coast of Sicily in 1718. At a conference in Madrid, a plan was made for an invasion of Britain on two fronts, using Spanish ships, troops, and arms. The Pretender was to sail with the main fleet – 30 ships under the command of the duke of Ormonde – and land in England, where it was hoped that several thousand supporters would rally to the cause. The smaller fleet – three ships, commanded by Earl Marischal Keith and his brother James Keith – was to land in Scotland.

The main fleet did not set sail for England. In March 1719, most of the ships, which were supposed to assemble at Coruna, were lost in storms en route from Cadiz.

The leaders of the smaller fleet, which set sail from San Sebastian, were unaware of the fate of Ormonde's fleet until they landed on the Scottish mainland. The earl marischal was determined that the Scottish rising should still continue, and placed a garrison of 45 Spanish troops in Eilean Donan Castle, guarding munitions and supplies. His intention was to rally support from the Seaforth Mackenzies and then to progress towards Inverness. Before the enterprise had got under way, disaster struck.

The battle of Glen Shiel

A small fleet of British ships sailed into Loch Alsh, destroyed Eilean Donan Castle and captured the Spanish garrison. The earl marischal's force was left without supplies or adequate arms, but his retreat had effectively been cut off and he was faced with no alternative but to proceed inland. The small Spanish force that he had brought with him had been swelled by Mackenzie and MacGregor clansmen, but he still had little more than 1000 men at his command. As his men advanced through Glen Shiel, between Loch Duich and Loch Cluanie, they were intercepted by a British force led by General Wightman. What followed was hardly a battle. There would be no gallant charge of Highlanders – as the British artillery tore into their ranks with a vengeance it quickly became clear that there could be no victory for the Jacobites. The earl marischal and other leaders managed to escape. The Scottish contingent of the invasion force dispersed and headed for home. The Spaniards, with nowhere to go and nothing left to fight for, gave themselves up for capture. The Jacobites did not rise again for another 25 years.

BATTLE OF PRESTONPANS,
21 SEPTEMBER 1745

The rising of 1745

The French government had not offered any substantial support to the Jacobite cause since the abortive rising of 1708, but in 1744, with France and Britain in conflict once again, Louis XV decided upon a plan for an invasion of England with Charles Edward Stewart, son of the Pretender, in command. Charles left Rome shortly after New Year, 1744, and travelled to France. The plan was for a fleet of 22 warships, sailing from Brest, to distract the British fleet, while a second fleet of transport ships, carrying 15,000 soldiers and Charles Edward Stewart, sailed from Dunkirk to England. The plan foundered in the early stages of its execution. The warships were unable to evade the British fleet, and only narrowly escaped total destruction. The transport ships met with stormy weather not far out of Dunkirk and more than half of them sank. The invasion was abandoned and the French refused further active support for the Jacobites.

Charles Edward Stewart was unwilling to give up hope of regaining the throne for the Stewarts. He was determined to sail to Scotland, with or without the help of the French. By the summer of the following year he had raised enough funds to charter two ships and set sail on 5 July with seven companions. When he landed at Eriskay, he had only one ship. The other vessel, the *Elizabeth,* carrying money and munitions, had been forced to turn back after being attacked by an English warship.

The young prince's arrival was not met with overwhelming optimism or enthusiasm – the general feeling among the Highland chiefs, however loyal they might be to the Stewart cause, was that a rising without the support of the French could not possibly succeed. But the young prince was persistent and persuasive and had soon managed to enlist the support of Cameron of Lochiel and Alexander Macdonald. When the Stewart standard was raised at Glenfinnan on 19 August, Charles had rallied almost 1000 supporters, most of whom were Camerons and Macdonalds.

The progress of the Jacobites was rapid. The government army led by Sir John Cope, numbering less than 2000 men, marched north towards the centre of the Highlands, but then chose to avoid an encounter with Charles's army and turned northeast, to Inverness. The Jacobites were then able to proceed unhindered to Perth and occupy the town. Their numbers were growing – they now numbered more than 2000 men – and at Perth, Charles found two valuable military leaders to support his cause – the duke of Perth and Lord George Murray.

Cope had put his army to sea from Inverness and was sailing towards the Forth. The race was now on to gain the capital. From Perth, the prince led his army across the Forth close to Stirling and marched towards Edinburgh. In Edinburgh there was a garrison of government troops occupying the castle, but the city itself was poorly guarded. A regiment of dragoons under Colonel Gardiner, which had failed to prevent Charles's passage across the Forth, was posted at Coltbridge to the west of the city. The City Guard, a force of around 600 men, composed of veterans and hastily summoned, untrained volunteers, was unlikely to be able to put up any resistance. On 16 September, as the Jacobite army approached Edinburgh, the dragoons at Coltbridge melted back into the city. The City Guard was disbanded before it had to strike a blow. On 17 September, early in the morning, Lord George Murray and

Cameron of Lochiel led their men through the city gates. Charles entered the city soon after and occupied Holyrood Palace. Only the castle held out against the occupying army. At the Mercat Cross in the centre of the city, Charles's father was proclaimed king of Great Britain and Ireland.

With Edinburgh in his possession, Charles now had to deal with Cope's army, which had landed at Dunbar and was now advancing towards the city. Charles led an army of 2500 men out of Edinburgh on 19 September, ready for a confrontation with Cope. The two armies came together at Prestonpans on 20 September.

The battle of Prestonpans

Cope had chosen his site carefully before assembling his force in battle order. To the north was the Firth of Forth. To the south the land had a good cover of shrubs and trees, and the added protection of extensive marshland to the south and southeast. Charles's army, facing him from a position close to Tranent, lying to the south, would be unable to make an effective charge. Cope's army, although no bigger than Charles's, was well-equipped with artillery, which would further hamper a head-long attack. Some other strategy would have to be worked out for the Jacobites to have a chance of victory.

In the event, they were helped by a man (one Robert Anderson) who had local knowledge and was able to lead the way along a narrow path through the marsh that protected Cope's front. Under cover of darkness, the Jacobite army picked its way in single file along the pathway, and having crossed the marsh, moved to a position to the east of Cope's left flank. The manoeuvre was only discovered when it was almost complete. Cope could do nothing but turn his army to face east, where the enemy now had the advantage.

Cope drew his army up with infantry in the centre, artillery on the right, and dragoons on each wing. His men had the rising sun in their eyes and were disconcerted by the sudden change of position. A burst of artillery fire from Cope's side started the battle, but the Highlanders were in no mood to wait to be shot down. They launched a furious charge, giving no time for enemy guns to be reloaded, no time for bayonets to be brought into play. Instantly, panic broke out in Cope's army. The dragoons wheeled around and fled. The men manning the cannons abandoned their positions and ran for their lives. The infantry could not hold out against the force of the charge either. Cope's attempts to rally his men into order to fight back against the claymore-wielding furies that beset them were in vain. More than 500 of Cope's men were killed by the charge or as they tried to flee. More than 1000 were taken prisoner. Cope himself managed to escape with a company of horsemen, shamed by the defeat. Compared to the heavy losses suffered by their enemies, casualties among the Highlanders were light. Charles led his army back to Edinburgh in triumph. Scotland was at his feet.

BATTLE OF FALKIRK,
17 JANUARY 1746

Advance and retreat

Charles stayed in Edinburgh for five weeks. During this period he was rearming and resupplying his army, but time was also spent in celebration and merrymaking. The period of inaction could not go on, however. The longer he waited the more he risked losing valuable soldiers in his army. The clansmen were accustomed to returning to their homelands after battle, not waiting in idleness and uncertainty. Moreover, the success of the Jacobites' campaign so far had been in part due to the limited manpower that could be rallied to oppose them, with a large part of George II's army occupied on the Continent. Now reinforcements were being called back to England. An army under General Wade was marching north via Newcastle, and further south a second army under the duke of Cumberland had been assembled and was also on the move from London. The prince believed that an advance into England would enable him to rouse the English Jacobites into action on his behalf. He also felt confident that such a move would bring French support, which had been promised after Prestonpans but had not yet materialised.

The decision to invade England did not meet with universal agreement – Lord George Murray, the most able military strategist amongst Charles's leaders, was one of those who argued against it – but the prince had his way. At the beginning of November, he led an army of 5000 men out of Edinburgh to begin the advance towards London by the western route. They reached Carlisle without any difficulty and the town surrendered. Wade's army, outmanoeuvred and outpaced, could not catch up with the Jacobite force, which pressed on to Manchester unopposed. In Manchester, they gathered a few hundred more men, but their situation was becoming more dangerous. Wade was following them from the north, and to the south Cumberland's army of 8000 men was advancing through Staffordshire. Nonetheless, Charles's army turned southeast, evaded Cumberland, and reached Derby safely.

It was only at this point, less than 130 miles from London, that the doubts expressed by Murray and the clan leaders in Edinburgh turned to certainty that the invasion was doomed. The advance into England had been successful as far as it had gone, but supplies and money were running low and there was still no word of help on its way from France. They were deep in enemy territory and had not yet managed to rally any significant degree of support from the English Jacobites. Now winter was closing in. In spite of the prince's protestations, his leaders refused to continue the advance. On 6 December 1745, the Jacobite army turned and began the long and perilous retreat northwards. It took them only two weeks to return to Scotland – the speed of the retreat is a testament to the hardiness and determination of the Highland clansmen when faced with adversity. The efforts of Cumberland and Wade to prevent them reaching Scottish soil were to no avail. Cumberland's army could not catch up with them. Wade was unable to block their way across the border. Apart from one brief skirmish between Cumberland's advance guard and the Jacobite rear at Clifton near Penrith, the Jacobites reached Scotland unhindered.

The battle of Falkirk

After the Jacobite army had reached Scotland, they proceeded to Glasgow and then in the early days of the new year, to

Stirling, where they laid siege to the castle. Their numbers were increasing again – reinforcements gathered by Viscount Strathallan and Lord John Drummond had come down from the north, swelling the size of the army at Stirling to approximately 8000 men.

The duke of Cumberland had been recalled to the south of England and Lieutenant-General Hawley was placed in command of the royal army. With a force almost equal in size to that of the Jacobites, Hawley was now advancing from Edinburgh to relieve Stirling Castle. He reached Falkirk and set up camp there while he gathered intelligence on the Jacobite army and planned his strategy. When Charles heard of Hawley's advance, the decision was taken to attack rather than wait for Hawley's next move. The Jacobite army moved out of its base at Bannockburn on 17 January. Hawley's army, hastily assembled into order after hearing of the Jacobite advance, struggled to reach higher ground but were beaten to it by the more nimble Highlanders.

It was a stormy afternoon, and the light was fading. A southwesterly wind was blowing in the faces of the royal army, wetting the powder in their muskets as they faced their enemy, little more than 100 yards away. Hawley gave the command to his dragoons, who were drawn up on the left of his line, to charge. The Highlanders responded with a volley of musket fire and almost at once the dragoons were in disarray. The right wing of the Highland army then dropped their muskets and charged Hawley's infantry. The first line was driven back against the second line and very swiftly the second line was also broken and the soldiers in flight, pursued by the Highlanders. The rout would have been complete had it not been for the efforts of the soldiers on the right wing of the royal army, where the Highlanders' assault had not been so strong. They held off their attackers with considerable courage and it was not until some of the Highlanders were called back from pursuing the fugitives to rejoin the battle that Hawley was forced to concede a total defeat. With no time to strike camp, he ordered the tents to be burned before the retreat and leaving the artillery and supplies for the enemy to claim, headed for Linlithgow.

Hawley's force had lost almost 300 men. No more than 50 Jacobites had been killed. Charles's army might have counted the victory a greater one if they had pursued Hawley as he retreated. They had won the battle, but they had not significantly diminished the threat that still hung over them.

BATTLE OF CULLODEN, 16 APRIL 1746

From Falkirk to Culloden

After the battle of Falkirk, the Jacobite forces resumed the siege of Stirling Castle, but after only a few days Charles came under pressure to move again. Large numbers of his Highland followers were disappearing and his army now numbered little more than 5000 men. The duke of Cumberland, who was now in overall command of the royal army, had assembled a force of more than 10,000 men and would soon be making a move against them. The clan chiefs were pressing hard for a retreat north, where they would find it easier to evade Cumberland's troops and where they believed they would be able to muster enough additional support to double the size of their army. Although Charles was strongly against such a move, he was forced to acquiesce.

The Jacobite army withdrew from Stirling shortly before Cumberland's arrival at the end of January. They crossed the Forth at Frew and headed for Perth, where they split into two sections to continue the journey towards Inverness. Charles led the first directly north, via Crieff, while Murray led his men towards the east coast and Aberdeen before heading north and west for Inverness. With Inverness as the centre of operations, the Jacobites engaged in a number of minor enterprises in the next few weeks. They laid siege to Fort William. Fort Augustus was taken, Loudon's men were driven out of Dornoch and there were a number of successful skirmishes in

Speyside. Lord George Murray led a body of men to besiege Blair Castle, but was unable to capture it. Throughout this period, the Jacobite army was finding it increasingly difficult to get hold of adequate supplies of food. Money and supplies had been dispatched from France, but an effective English blockade prevented any of the ships from landing. With little food and no money to purchase more, the Jacobites were forced to forage for what they could find in the surrounding countryside. Cumberland's army, well supplied with stores from a fleet of ships off the east coast, had settled in Aberdeen, where Cumberland was content to wait for the weather to improve before making his move.

In the second week of April, Cumberland's army advanced out of Aberdeen and on 14 April, set up camp at Nairn, less than 15 miles from the Jacobite army. Cumberland had more than 9000 men with him. With large numbers of his army either absent on expeditions or having gone home, Charles could barely count 5000 in his force. Desperation was beginning to set in and Charles made up his mind to face Cumberland in battle. The site he chose, Drumossie Moor by Culloden House, could not have been less favourable for the Highland style of fighting, nor more favourable for the royalists. It was open moorland, where there would be no cover for a Highland charge. The Hanoverian army, which was vastly superior in artillery, would have a clear range for its guns. The Scots army took up position on Drumossie Moor on 15 April, ready for battle, but as the day wore on, it became clear that Cumberland was not on his way. Cumberland's army was, in fact, still at Nairn, where the duke was taking a day of rest to celebrate his 25th birthday.

Towards the end of the day, the decision was taken to march on Cumberland's camp at Nairn by night and take the Hanoverians by surprise. By the time appointed for their departure, however, almost one-third of the army was absent, having gone off in search of food. Eventually 4000 or so were mustered. Hungry, tired, and discontented, they straggled in a disorderly train through the darkness, with Murray leading the vanguard. Their progress was slow and laborious, with the columns to the rear finding it hard to keep up with the front. It had been the plan to surprise Cumberland's men in the early hours of the morning while they slept, but they were not moving fast enough. The Jacobite leaders realised that it would be dawn before they were ready to attack, by which time their presence would have been discovered by Cumberland's sentries. Once again there was disagreement. While some felt it better to take their chances at Nairn rather than at Culloden where the site was so unfavourable, others wanted to return. Charles favoured the former option, Murray the latter. In the end, the decision was taken to return. The men were already very tired and had had virtually nothing to eat. By the time they had got back to Culloden, around six o'clock in the morning, they were almost on their knees with exhaustion and hunger. Some wandered off in a desperate search for food, whilst the others lay down in the open to get what little sleep they could. They would not be able to take their ease for long. Cumberland's army was on the move from Nairn at first light and was rapidly approaching.

The battle of Culloden

It was still well before noon when the warning went out that the Redcoats were in sight. Cumberland was not opting for the tactic of sudden attack. Unhurriedly, he assembled his men in battle formation on the moor and the men waited for their orders. The Jacobites had plenty of time to prepare themselves for the battle, but for those who had the foresight to envisage what lay ahead of them, the time must have felt like the last hours spent by a condemned man in his cell. When both armies were drawn up and ready, more time was taken to manoeuvre them into position, each side with one eye on the movements of the enemy. The leaders rode along the front of their lines, urging their men to give of their best. Cumberland's army was drawn up in two lines with a third held in reserve. The first line, three men deep, consisted of six regiments and the second had five. Four regiments made up the reserve. The prince's army was drawn up in similar fashion in two lines, but with a much smaller reserve. The Highlanders were in the front line, with the Macdonalds on the left, the Athol Highlanders on the right, and Camerons, Stuarts of Appin, Frasers, Mackintoshes, Chisholms, and others between. The cavalry were placed in the second line, some of them dismounted to fight as foot soldiers. Murray took command of the right of the field, Lord Drummond led the centre and the duke of Perth, the left. The prince placed himself at the right, a little way behind the front line.

The battle began some time after one o'clock in the afternoon, with artillery fire from both sides. The superiority of the Hanoverian guns quickly became obvious. Cumberland's artillery pounded the Jacobite ranks with deadly effect. The Jacobite cannons, on the other hand, lacked the range and accuracy necessary for the task that was expected of them and were soon abandoned. The Highlanders were not willing to withstand such a battering for long and were soon urging their leaders for the command to attack. Eventually, after 30 minutes or so, the Highlanders surged forward. The men of clan Mackintosh were the first to charge – according to some sources, they had not waited for the order to move. They were closely followed by the rest of the men from the right and centre.

Cumberland had prepared his army carefully to meet the terrors of the Highland charge. The men in the front line knelt with their muskets at the ready, waiting to fire until they could be sure of hitting their advancing targets. As the charge came closer, they relied on the men behind them to keep up continuous musket fire over their heads as they waited to use their bayonets. The clansmens' tactic was generally to fire one volley from their muskets and then, casting them aside, to charge with claymore in the right hand, dirk in the left. Their shields – targes – were worn on the left arm. Cumberland's men had been instructed, when the clansmen came within range of their bayonets, to strike not at the man immediately in front of them, but at the man to their right, thrusting the bayonet at or under the unprotected sword arm.

Hunger and fatigue seemed to have been forgotten as the Scots charged forward. Musket and cannon fire assailed them from in front and from the sides as they ran, and many fell before they had reached the English front line. They fought with tremendous bravery and managed to break through the first line but as they made for the second, it became clear that the advance was turning into a suicide mission. Too many had already fallen under the barrage of musket fire and the survivors were now hopelessly outnumbered. There were still many men in Charles's army who had not yet come into the battle and Cumberland's army was still not yet fully engaged, but it was clear that the Jacobites had no chance of succeeding. Cumberland's cavalry charged against the left wing of the Jacobite army and broke through it without any difficulty. When he sent his infantry in to follow up on the cavalry charge, the Jacobite army was put to flight. The prince was eager to rally them to fight on, but was advised that any attempt at fighting on would be futile. Against his will, he was persuaded to leave the field.

The battle itself had been bloody enough. Hundreds of Jacobites lay dead on the field, including almost all of those who had taken part in the charge. But the aftermath of the battle was devastating. Although some of the Jacobite army escaped southwards to Badenoch, many made for Inverness, only to be killed after a relentless pursuit by horsemen from Cumberland's army. In the weeks that followed, Cumberland followed a campaign of cruel reprisals. Prince Charles spent five months in the Highlands, hiding out from the government troops until he was able to find safe passage back to the Continent. There was a price on his head, but no one gave him up. His supporters meanwhile were being hunted down and punished mercilessly. The houses of Jacobite sympathisers were burned and the inhabitants dragged out to face their fates. Some spent long months languishing in prison before being taken for trial, after which they were sentenced to death or transportation. Others were killed on the spot. Cumberland was more interested in revenge than in justice, more concerned with stamping out his adversaries than with showing them mercy or leniency. The reprisals in the Highlands continued unabated until Cumberland left Scotland at the end of July.

The Jacobite cause was lost. In the course of the campaign of 1745, it had become clear that supporters of the Stewarts could not be rallied in sufficient numbers to fight unless they had adequate support from abroad. The French had hesitated to give Charles support at the outset. By the time finances and munitions had been sent, the English fleets, well warned, had successfully prevented them from reaching their destination. The victories that Charles had won in the early months of his campaign could not have been sustained – defeat had been inevitable from the start.

The Jacobite defeat at Culloden was also to mark the beginning of the end of the clan system in the Highlands. The government was determined to stamp out the threat of any future risings in the Highlands. A Disarming Act was passed and rigorously enforced, and the Gaelic language and the wearing of tartan and Highland dress were outlawed. The final blow came in 1748 when heritable jurisdictions were abolished. The clan chiefs lost their legal powers and authority – the leaders who had been able to call their men to fight for them at any time were now reduced to the status of landlord.